The CREEDAL
IMPERATIVE

The CREEDAL
IMPERATIVE

CARL R. TRUEMAN

CROSSWAY
WHEATON, ILLINOIS

Cover design: Studio Gearbox

Cover images: Thinkstock

Interior design and typesetting: Lakeside Design Plus

First printing 2012

Printed in the United States of America

Trade Paperback ISBN: 978-1-4335-2190-4
PDF ISBN: 978-1-4335-2191-1
Mobipocket ISBN: 978-1-4335-2192-8
ePub ISBN: 978-1-4335-2193-5

Library of Congress Cataloging-in-Publication Data
Trueman, Carl R.
    The creedal imperative / Carl R. Trueman.
        p.   cm.
    Includes bibliographical references and index.
    ISBN 978-1-4335-2190-4 (tp)
    1. Creeds. I. Title.
BT990.T78   2012
238—dc23   2012013405

Crossway is a publishing ministry of Good News Publishers.

VP		21	20	19	18	17	16	15	14
14	13	12	11	10	9	8	7	6	5	4	3

Dedicated with gratitude to the students and friends
at Cornerstone Presbyterian Church
who have attended the monthly "Tabletalk at the Truemans'"
over the years, where many of the ideas in this book
were debated and refined.

Contents

Acknowledgments

I wish to thank Allan Fisher and Justin Taylor at Crossway for encouraging me in this project and waiting patiently as I missed a couple of deadlines. At Westminster, I have benefited from conversations about the nature of confessionalism with my friends, Sandy Finlayson, Greg Beale, Peter Lillback, Dick Gaffin, and David Garner. I must also thank Catriona, John, and Peter for providing such a happy home and escape from work.

Introduction

A colleague of mine loves to tell the following story about a church he used to visit. The pastor there had a habit of standing in the pulpit, seizing his Bible in his right hand, raising it above his head, and pointing to it with his left. "This," he declared in a booming voice, "is our only creed and our only confession." Ironically, the church was marked by teaching that included the five points of Calvinism, dispensationalism, and a form of polity that reflected in broad terms its origins as a Plymouth Brethren assembly. In other words, while its only creed was the Bible, it actually connected in terms of the details of its life and teaching to almost no other congregation in the history of the church. Clearly, the church did have a creed, a summary view of what the Bible taught on grace, eschatology, and ecclesiology; it was just that nobody ever wrote it down and set it out in public. That is a serious problem. As I shall argue in subsequent pages, it is actually unbiblical; and that is ironic and somewhat sad, given the (no doubt) sincere desire of the pastor and the people of this church to have an approach to church life that guaranteed the unique status of the Bible.

The burden that motivates my writing of this book is my belief that creeds and confessions are vital to the present and future well-being of the church. Such a statement may well jar with evangelical ears that are used to the notion that Scripture alone is to be considered the sole, supreme authority for Christian faith and practice. Does my claim not strike at the very heart of the notion of Scripture alone? Does it not place me in jeopardy of regarding both Scripture and something outside Scripture, some tradition, as being of coordinate and potentially equal authority? And is there not a danger that commitment to time-bound creeds and confessions might well doom the church to irrelevance in the modern world?

These are, indeed, legitimate concerns, and I intend to address these, and more, in the coming pages. Here, however, I want to place my own cards on the table. Every author writes from a particular perspective, with arguments shaped to some extent by personal commitments, background, and belief. Thus, it seems entirely appropriate to allow the reader insight into my own context and predispositions in order to be better prepared to understand what I am going to say.

I am a professor at a confessional Presbyterian seminary, Westminster in Philadelphia, and a minister in a confessional Presbyterian denomination, the Orthodox Presbyterian Church. In other words, I am a confessional Presbyterian. The terms "confessional" and "Presbyterian" are crucial for understanding both institutions. To take the latter term first, "Presbyterian" means that I am committed to a Presbyterian form of church government, whereby the church is ruled at a congregational level by a session, or committee, of elders; at a regional level by a presbytery of ministers and elders drawn from the churches in the area; and at a national level by a General Assembly of ministers and elders drawn from all parts of the country. When I became a minister in my denomination, I took vows to uphold this form of government both in what I teach and in the respect I give to the various courts of the church.

More significant for this book is the adjective "confessional." This means that I am committed to the idea that the Presbyterian confessional position, as stated in the Westminster Standards, represents a summary of the teaching of the Bible on key points such as who God is, who Christ is, what justification means, and so on. When I became a minister, I took a solemn vow to that effect. This points to another aspect of being confessional: my vows connect to a structure of church government such that, if I am found to be teaching something inconsistent with what I am pledged to uphold, I can be held to account. If necessary, in the worst situations, I can even be removed from public office in the church.

Notice, I said above that my vow reflects the fact that I believe the statements in the Westminster Standards are a summary of Scripture's teaching, not that I believe the Westminster Standards to represent teaching supplemental to Scripture, or independent of it. Rather, they summarize what is already there in Scripture itself.

Now, this position is not without its problems. How, one might ask, do I avoid making the Standards a kind of *a priori* framework into which Scripture is made to fit? In other words, is there not a danger here of tail wagging dog, of treating the summary as the grid by which I read Scripture? I will address these, and similar, questions later. At this point, my purpose is simply to let readers know the position that I occupy so they can understand the perspective from which this book is being written. In sum, I not only believe that creeds and confessions are good for the church, I am also committed by vow to uphold the teaching of a particular confession. This indicates that the status of creeds and confessions is not for me simply a matter of intellectual interest; I am committed to the notion at a deep, personal level.

The fact that I am a confessional Christian places me at odds with the vast majority of evangelical Christians today. That is ironic, because most Christian churches throughout the ages have defined themselves by commitment to some form of creed, confession, or doctrinal statement. This is the case for the Eastern Orthodox, for Roman Catholics, and for Lutheran, Reformed, and Anglican Protestants. Some streams of Baptists have also had confessions; and many independent churches today that may not think of themselves as confessional have brief statements of faith that define who they are and what they believe. Furthermore, as I shall argue later, even those churches and Christians who repudiate the whole notion of creeds and confessions will yet tend to operate with an implicit creed.

Despite this, it is true to say that we live in an anticonfessional age, at least in intention if not always in practice. The most blatant examples of this come from those who argue that the Protestant notion of Scripture alone simply requires the rejection of creeds and confessions. Scripture is the sole authority; of what use therefore are further documents? And how can one ever claim such documents have authority without thus derogating from the authority of Scripture? These arguments have a

15

certain specious force, but I will argue in chapters 1 and 2 that, while the reasons for anticonfessionalism are manifold, many of them are driven more by cultural forces of which too many are unaware. Awareness of these forces, by contrast, may not automatically free us from their influence but can at least offer us the opportunity of subjecting them to critique.

I do want to make the point here that Christians are not divided between those who have creeds and confessions and those who do not; rather, they are divided between those who have public creeds and confessions that are written down and exist as public documents, subject to public scrutiny, evaluation, and critique, and those who have private creeds and confessions that are often improvised, unwritten, and thus not open to public scrutiny, not susceptible to evaluation and, crucially and ironically, not, therefore, subject to testing by Scripture to see whether they are true.

Anticonfessionalism among evangelicals is actually closely related to their putative rejection of tradition. For many, the principle of Scripture alone stands against any notion that the church's tradition plays any constructive role in her life or thought. Some regard this as one of the principal insights of the Protestant Reformers: Rome had (and has) tradition; Protestantism has Scripture. The sixteenth-century Reformation was thus a struggle over authority, with church tradition being pitted against the supremacy of Scripture; and modern evangelicals stand in lockstep with their Protestant forebears on this matter.

A few moments of reflection, however, indicate how misleading and, in fact, untrue is the claim that Protestants have the Bible rather than tradition. Most evangelicals, for example, will typically use Bible translations, and such translations, be they the NIV, RSV, ESV, or KJV, stand within established traditions of Bible translation, linguistics, lexicography, etc. Further, beneath these translations lie the original Hebrew and Greek texts; so traditions of textual understanding also underlie these translations and, even for those linguistic geniuses who are more comfortable with just the Hebrew and Greek, these various traditions will shape the choice of text, the way the languages were learned, and the kind of choices made on matters of obscure grammar, syntax, and vocabulary. Thus, "Scripture alone," whatever else it means, cannot mean Scripture approached in a vacuum.

And we can take this reflection on tradition a step further. All Protestant pastors, even the most fundamentalist, will, if they are remotely competent, prepare their sermons with the help of lexicons, commentaries, and books of theology. As soon as they take down one of these books from their bookcases and start to read it, of course, they are drawing positively on church tradition. They are not simply reading the Word of God; they are reading the thoughts and reflections on that Word offered by someone else and articulated using words, sentences, and paragraphs that are not found anywhere in the Bible. Indeed, as soon as one uses the word "Trinity" from the pulpit, one is drawing on tradition, not Scripture.

In fact, *tradition* is not the issue; it is how one defines that tradition, and how one understands the way it connects to Scripture, which are really the points at issue. Indeed, this was the crux of the Reformation, which was not so much a struggle between Scripture and tradition as between different types of traditions. In a famous exchange between a leading light of the Catholic Reformation, Cardinal Sadoleto, and the Reformer, John Calvin, Sadoleto argued that the Protestants had abandoned the church tradition. Calvin responded that, on the contrary, the Protestants had the true tradition; it was the Catholic Church that had moved away from the truth. The point was simple and well-made: the tradition that transmitted the correct understanding of Scripture from generation to generation belonged to the Protestants.

Here is not the place to debate the veracity of Calvin's claim regarding the content of tradition; suffice it to note that he understood the Reformation not as Scripture versus tradition but as scriptural tradition versus unscriptural tradition. Thoughtful Protestants then, and ever since, have understood the Reformers as arguing for what we might call a tradition that is *normed* by Scripture. In other words, Protestants know that they use language and conceptual terminology not found explicitly in the Bible; but they understand such are useful in understanding what Scripture says and, at the point where they are found to be inadequate for this task, or even to contradict Scripture, there they must be modified or abandoned.

The same is true of the creeds and confessions of the church, which are, one might say, the most concentrated deposits of tradition, as affirmed by the church. These documents are often referred to as *normed norms* or, to use the Latin, *norma normata*, in contrast to Scripture which is the *norming norm*, or *norma normans*. What that means is that the creeds and confessions represent a public statement of what a particular church or denomination believes that Scripture teaches in a synthetic form. By synthetic, I do not mean "false," as in, say, a synthetic fiber like nylon, which is designed to look like cotton but is not really cotton. I mean rather a presentation that is not simply a collection of Bible verses but rather a thematic summary of what the Bible teaches. Thus, in the Nicene Creed, we have an explication of the identity of God as Father, Son, and Holy Spirit, which is considered to represent what the Bible as a whole teaches on this subject. The important point to note is that such statements are public, and thus open to public scrutiny in the light of what Scripture teaches. Thus, they can be accepted or rejected, modified or clarified, as and when they are found to be wanting; the context and means for such change we will discuss elsewhere. Here, I simply want the reader to note the synthetic and public nature of the documents.

This book consists of six chapters. In chapter 1, I look at some of the powerful currents within modern culture that serve to make the whole idea of creeds and confessions somewhat implausible. I do not intend to reduce evangelical objections to such secular forces, but I believe that an understanding of such forces can be of great help in clarifying why the case for confessionalism can be difficult to make at the present time.

In chapter 2, I look at the biblical teaching on a number of related points (the importance of language, the reality and unity of human nature, Paul's emphasis on doctrine, on eldership, on a "form of sound words," and on tradition). My conclusion is not only that creeds and confessions are plausible, given biblical teaching, but that Paul actually seems to assume that something like them will be a normal part of the postapostolic church's life. In other words, there is a sense in which the claim to have no creed but the Bible is incoherent, given the fact that the Bible itself seems to teach the need for creeds.

In chapter 3, I outline the ecclesiological developments of relevance to the case for creeds and confessions. In particular, I focus on the Trinitarian/christological discussions between the Council of Nicaea in 325 and the Council of Chalcedon in 451. I also touch on the Apostles' and the Athanasian creeds. Two important lessons I draw from this study relate to doctrinal complexity and the importance of the church. As to the former, history teaches that many Christian doctrines can only exist in a stable form within a relatively complex network of related doctrines. Christian theology, in other words, always has a certain ineradicable complexity, which has serious implications for the modern evangelical predilection for simple and very brief statements of faith. As to ecclesiology, it is clear from the early church that terms such as "heresy" really only have a meaningful content when connected to a church that has a specific confession.

In chapter 4, I deal with major Protestant confessional standards: the Anglican Articles and Homilies; the Lutheran Book of Concord; the Three Forms of Unity; the Westminster Standards; and the 1689 Baptist Confession of Faith. This chapter is of necessity highly selective. Protestantism has produced a vast amount of confessional material, and so I have chosen to focus on those with which I am most familiar. In choosing these, I do not intend to imply that Arminians, General Baptists, Anabaptists, and others do not have confessions and cannot be confessional. I hope that anyone from these traditions who reads this book will see that the principles of confessionalism are not confined simply to those confessions I happen to have mentioned.

In chapter 5, in order to do justice to the doxological origins of Christian creeds and to underline the important function that such have played, and can continue to play, in the life of the church, I focus on creeds and praise. Too often we think of these documents in a negative sense, as if their sole purpose was simply to keep people out of the church and to offer a dry-as-dust account of the Christian faith. By contrast, creeds are central to Christian doxology.

In chapter 6, I make the case for the usefulness of confessions by highlighting a number of advantages to having them, from limitation of church power to a proper pedagogical structure for church life.

After the conclusion, I also include an appendix, addressing the vexing question of the possibility and practicality of confessional revision.

In writing this book, I come to my subject as one convinced that confessional Christianity captures a very important aspect of biblical teaching on the church. I was an evangelical for many years; discovering confessional Presbyterianism in my early thirties was a liberating experience. Nevertheless, I am aware that there can be a rather distasteful, not to mention sinful, tendency among many confessional writers to look down with scorn and derision on those who are not confessional. I trust that I have not written in that spirit; rather, I hope that this book will go some way to persuading nonconfessional Christians who love the Bible and seek to follow Christ that confessionalism, far from being something to fear, can actually help them to better protect that which is so dear to them.

The astute reader should now be able to see the case I want to make in this book: I want to argue that creeds and confessions are thoroughly consistent with the belief that Scripture alone is the unique source of revelation and authority. Indeed, I want to go somewhat further: I want to argue that creeds and confessions are, in fact, necessary for the well-being of the church, and that churches that claim not to have them place themselves at a permanent disadvantage when it comes to holding fast to that form of sound words which was so precious to the aging Paul as he advised his young protégé, Timothy. Linked to this latter point, I want to make the case that it is at least arguable, based on Scripture, that the need for creeds and confessions is not just a practical imperative for the church but is also a biblical imperative.

1

The Cultural Case against Creeds and Confessions

In the introduction, I briefly mentioned the standard, knee-jerk reaction against creeds and confessions, often found in evangelical circles, that such documents supplant the unique place of the Bible, place tradition on an equal—or even superior—footing with Scripture, and thus compromise a truly evangelical, Protestant notion of authority. While I will offer a more thorough response to this line of objection later, I did note that all Christians engage in confessional synthesis; the difference is simply whether one adheres to a public confession, subject to public scrutiny, or to a private confession that is, by its very nature, immune to such examination.

Before proceeding to a more thoroughgoing exposition of the use and the usefulness of confessions, however, it is worth spending some time reflecting on other reasons why creeds and confessions are regarded with such suspicion these days. While the objection to them is often couched in language that appears to be jealous for biblical authority, there are also powerful forces at work within our modern world that militate against adherence to historic statements of the Christian faith. As the goldfish swimming in the bowl is unaware of the temperature and taste of the water in which he swims, so often the most powerfully formative forces of our societies and cultures are those with which we are so familiar as to be functionally unaware of how they shape our thinking, even our thinking about what exactly it means to say that Scripture has supreme and unique authority. It would be a tragic irony if the rejection of creeds and confessions by so many of those who sincerely wish to be biblically faithful turned out to be not an act of faithfulness but rather an unwitting capitulation to the spirit of the age. It is some of the forces that shape this spirit that I address in this chapter.

Three Assumptions

My conviction that creeds and confessions are a good and necessary part of healthy, biblical church life rests on a host of different arguments and convictions; but, at root, there are three basic presuppositions to which I hold that must be true for the case for confessions to be a sound one. These are as follows:

1. *The past is important, and has things of positive relevance to teach us.* Creeds and confessions are, almost by definition, documents that were composed at some point in the past; and, in most cases, we are talking about the distant past, not last week or last year. Thus, to claim that creeds and confessions still fulfill positive functions, in terms of transmitting truth from one generation to another or making it clear to the outside world what it is that particular churches believe, requires that we believe the past can still speak to us today. Thus, any cultural force that weakens or attenuates the belief that the past can be a source of knowledge and even wisdom is also a force that serves to undermine the relevance of creeds and confessions.

2. *Language must be an appropriate vehicle for the stable transmission of truth across time and geographical space.* Creeds and confessions are documents that make theological truth claims. That is not to say that that is *all* that they do: the role, for example, of the Apostles' and the Nicene creeds in many church liturgies indicates that they can also fulfill doxological as well as pedagogical and theological roles; but while they can thus be more, they can never be less than theological, doctrinal statements that rest upon and express truth claims about God and the world he has created. They do this, of course, in words; and

so, if these claims are to be what they claim to be—statements about a reality beyond language—then language itself must be an adequate medium for performing this task. Thus, any force that undermines general confidence in language as a medium capable of conveying information or of constituting relationships is also a force that strikes at the validity of creeds and confessions.

3. *There must be a body or an institution that can authoritatively compose and enforce creeds and confessions.* This body or institution is the church. I will address the significance of this in more detail in subsequent chapters, but it is important to understand at the outset that confessions are not private documents. They are significant because they have been adopted by the church as public declarations of her faith, and their function cannot be isolated from their ecclesiastical nature and context. This whole concept assumes that institutions and institutional authority structures are not necessarily bad or evil or defective simply by their very existence as institutions. Thus, any cultural force that overthrows or undermines notions of external or institutional authority effectively removes the mechanisms by which creeds and confessions can function as anything other than simple summaries of doctrine for private edification.

If these are the presuppositions of confessionalism, then it is clear that we have a major problem, because each of these three basic presuppositions represents a profoundly countercultural position, something that stands opposed to the general flow of modern life. Today, the past is more often a source of embarrassment than a positive source of knowledge; and when it is considered useful, it is usually as providing examples of what not to do or of defective, less advanced thinking than of truth for the present. Language is similarly suspect: in a world of spin, dishonest politicians, and ruthless marketing, language can often seem to be—indeed, often is—manipulative, deceptive, or downright wicked, but rarely transparent and something to be taken at face value. Then, finally, institutions, from multinational corporations to governments, seem to be in the game of self-perpetuation, bullying, and control for the sake of control. They are never seen as entities that exist in practice for the real benefit of others. Thus, the big three presuppositions of confessionalism fly in the face of the values of contemporary culture, and confessionalists clearly have their work cut out to mount a counterattack. And such a counterattack begins with the simple truism of every successful campaigner, from wartime leaders to the coaches of high school track teams: know your enemy. In this context, knowing the enemy may also help us to realize how, in our defense of the unique authority of Scripture, our understanding of what that means is sometimes shaped more by the hidden forces of the world around us than by the teaching of Scripture and the historic life and practice of the church.

Devaluing the Past

Science

Numerous forces within modern culture serve to erode any notion that the past might be a useful source of wisdom. Perhaps the most obvious is the dominance of science. I am not, of course, referring to the content of science. Science undergirds almost all of those things which make life bearable, from electric lightbulbs to cancer treatment. To say science is the enemy is not, in this instance, to be antiscience. Rather, I am thinking of the kind of cultural mindset that science helps to cultivate and reinforce.

Science, by its very nature, assumes that the present is better than the past and the future will be better than the present. Again, this is not in itself a bad thing. It is surely part of what drives the laudable curiosity that motivates scientists and leads to major breakthroughs; and there is much evidence that this—the fact the present is better than the past—is, indeed, the case. As one who teaches history, I am often asked by students in which period of history I would most have enjoyed living. My answer is simple and straightforward: this one, the here and now. Call me a weakling if you like, but I would much rather live in an era with analgesics, antibiotics, and flush toilets than in earlier periods where pain killers were unknown, medicine usually involved swallowing some kill-or-cure snake oil made by a wrinkled old crone with dubious personal hygiene, and the "facilities" were little more than a hole in the ground on the edge of the village. By and large, in areas where it is relevant, science has made the world a better place.

The evidence is not all one way, however: the Holocaust, for example, is one instance where science was clearly used to destroy rather than enhance life, and that on a huge scale. But, by and large, science has brought with it huge gains, from medicine to dishwashers.

The problem is that science also comes loaded with a certain philosophical bias, and that is, as stated above, that the past is inferior to the present. It has a built-in narrative of progress, whereby everything—or at least almost everything—just keeps getting better; and the problem is that this tends to inculcate a broader cultural attitude that applies the same kind of expectation in other areas. Throw concepts like evolution into the mix, and you have a gravitational pull within the culture toward the future, built on the assumed inferiority of the past.

This narrative of scientific progress instills a belief not simply in the superiority of the present in relation to the past but also in its uniqueness. This time in which we live has so much more knowledge, displays so much more sophistication, and is so much more complicated than the past. Thus that past is consequently of no real use in addressing the problems or issues of the present, so great is the difference between them. One would not, for example, use a horse and cart to transport fuel from an oil refinery to a petrol station. Nor would one today consult a seventeenth-century textbook on surgery to find out how to remove a burst appendix. So why would one turn to some confession written in the fourth or the seventeenth century to find a summary guide to what Christians today should believe?

Some years ago, I was exposed to precisely this attitude while teaching a class on the ancient church. At some point, I mentioned that a certain professor from another institution was going to be visiting campus to deliver some lectures on the Westminster Standards, that is, the Confession and the Larger and Shorter Catechisms. A student immediately asked why she should bother attending these because "some documents written in the seventeenth century seem to have very little to do with" her ministry. I asked her if she had read these apparently irrelevant documents recently. She said she had not. I then pointed out to her that these documents had been regarded by many people as vital and vibrant expressions of the Christian faith since their composition. Given this, and their connection to historic traditions and trajectories of church life and Christian thought, I suggested with every ounce of tact and gentleness I could muster that she might perhaps better ask herself not so much what relevance they have to her ministry but what relevance her ministry had to the church. Her assumption was simple: the past could not really speak in any meaningful way to the present. She was truly a child of the scientific age.

Technology

Closely related to the role of science in cultivating an attitude that downgrades the importance of the past is that of technology. A simple example should make this point clear. My mother lives in an old weaver's cottage in the Cotswolds. In what is now her living room, there is a stone fireplace and, in that fireplace, there are a series of small holes, roughly an inch in diameter, now plugged with wood, which indicate where the weaver would have had his loom. It is easy to imagine a scene in the early nineteenth century in which the weaver was hard at work making cloth when one of his children wandered into the room and inquired as to what exactly he was doing. No doubt, the weaver would have sat the child down and explained how the loom operated, how the shuttle carried the woolen thread from one side to the other and slowly but surely formed a sheet of fabric. The flow of knowledge from the older generation to the younger was clear; this was no doubt repeated many times in preindustrial societies around the world, where children typically grew up to follow in the footsteps of their parents and were thus more or less apprenticed to their parents from an early age.

Now, jump forward nearly two hundred years to a scene in the same room. I am sitting there, trying to set up my mother's DVR to record a Gloucester versus Leicester rugby match and, try as I might, I cannot get the machine to do what I want it to do. In walks my niece and asks what I am trying to do. After I explain to her what is going on, she sighs, rolls her eyes, picks up the remote control, and with what seems to me to be two touches of the buttons, has the machine set up to record the match. With a shake of her head, she walks back into the kitchen.

Notice what has happened here, and what the significance of these two encounters is: the flow of knowledge has been reversed. No longer is the younger dependent upon the older; rather, the older is dependent upon the younger. Technology, because it is constantly and rapidly changing, inevitably favors those who have been brought up with it, and who have the kind of young, agile minds that develop new skills quickly and easily. You cannot easily teach a middle-aged historian, any more than an old dog, new tricks; and that means that technology will always favor the young.

This is just one anecdote and, as my secretary will tell you, I am among the more—ahem—technologically challenged men of my generation; but the general point is a good one. The technological world, particularly given the rapidity with which it is constantly changing, creates an environment where the assumption is that older people are going to be dependent upon the younger. Taken by itself, perhaps, this might not be so significant; but combined with the impact of science as a whole upon cultural attitudes, it undoubtedly plays its role in the bias against age, and thus against the past, which is a hallmark of the modern world and which is not incidental in the general antipathy among Christians for creeds and confessions.

Consumerism

A third cultural force that militates against respect for the past is consumerism. As with science, there is much that could be said here, but I will restrict myself to the most salient aspects of the phenomenon.

Consumerism can be defined as an over-attachment to material goods and possessions such that one's meaning or worth is determined by them. This definition is reasonably helpful but misses one key aspect of the phenomenon: it is not just the attachment to material things, it is also the need for constant acquisition of the same. Life is enriched not simply by possessing goods but by the process of acquiring them; consumerism is as much a function of boredom as it is of crass materialism.

What has this to do with rejection of the past? Simply this: consumerism is predicated on the idea that life can be fulfilling through acquiring something in the future that one does not have in the present. This manifests itself in the whole strategic nature of marketing. For example, every time you switch on your television set, you are bombarded with advertisements that may be for a variety of different goods and services but that all preach basically the same message: what you have now is not enough for happiness; you need something else, something new, in order to find true fulfillment. I believe that this reinforces fundamentally negative attitudes toward the past.

Think for a moment: how many readers of this book are wearing clothes they bought ten years ago? How many are using computers they bought five years ago? Or driving automobiles more than fifteen years old? With the exception of vintage car collectors, the economically poor, and those with absolutely no fashion sense, most readers will probably respond in the negative to at least one, if not all three, of these questions. Yet when we ask why this is the case, there is no sensible answer. We can put a man on the moon, so we could probably make an automobile that lasts for fifty years; most of us do little on computers that could not have been done on the machines we owned five years ago; and we all throw away clothes that still fit us and are quite presentable. So why the need for the new?

A number of factors influence this kind of behavior. First, there is the role of built-in obsolescence: it is not in the manufacturer's best interest to make a washing machine that will last for a hundred years. If that were done, then the manufacturer would likely be out of business within a decade as the market became saturated. Such is a possible, but actually unlikely, scenario. Developments in technology mean that longevity will not be the only factor driving the market. Efficiency, for example, or enhanced and multiplied functions might well create a continuing need for more goods. Aesthetics also play a role; the ability to market goods based on aesthetics and image has proved powerful. Remember the cool, sleek look that Apple computers developed at one point? That gave them a clear edge over their rivals.

Second, and related to the first point, we see in the consumer economy a coalescence of aesthetics and a bias to the young in the creation of the so-called youth market, and the closely related marketing of youth to older types like myself. If no eighteen-year-old male believes himself to be mortal, so no middle-aged male wants to appear to be any older than he was twenty years ago. Indeed, with the exception of those odd types (of the kind who read *The Daily Telegraph* in the UK and the *National Review* in the US) who were probably born with comb-overs, receding hairlines, and bottle glasses, it would seem that the market for youth clothing (albeit with slightly expanded waistline sizes) is alive and well long into territory previously reserved for the superannuated and beyond.

In today's topsy-turvy world, youth has status. That is why so many old-timers spend large amounts of money and time trying to hold on to, or even win back, some of its accoutrements, whether by purchasing a pair of jeans from Aeropostale, buying a male grooming kit, or even undergoing drastic plastic surgery. Harmless as these phenomena are at one level, at another they are part of the larger cultural impulse toward disdain for the past and for old age. We see this not just in fashion, of course, but also in the "wisdom" now invested in young people who are considered competent to opine on complex matters, not *despite* the fact of their relative youth and inexperience but precisely *because of* it. Pop music, a function of youth culture if ever there was one, is perhaps responsible for this. In the last few decades, we have had the pleasure of hearing all manner of people, from Hall & Oates in the eighties to Lady Gaga in the present, telling the world what to do about everything from apartheid to third world debt to gay marriage. Apparently, the lack of "baggage" (to use the standard pejorative) is an advantage to being able to speak with authority on complex subjects. In other professions, of course—from plumbing to brain surgery and beyond—"baggage" is generally referred to as "appropriate training," but, such is the power of a youthful smile, a full head of hair, and a trim waistline that such does not apply to matters of morality, economics, or the meaning of life in general.

As a postscript, the impact of consumerism is one reason why church sessions and elder boards often spend more time than is decent on discussions about worship and programs. Someone will make the point that certain young people have left because the worship is not to their liking and thus the church needs to think again about how it does things. Laying aside the fact that, for most of us, no church gives us everything we want in worship but we are nonetheless happy to attend because the Word is truly preached, it is interesting to note the session member's response: *we* need to do something, to think again about worship. In other words, we need to respond to the needs of the consumer. An alternative approach might be that we need to do a better job of explaining why we do what we do, and what the obligations entailed in solemn vows of membership are; yet this is often not the knee-jerk reaction to such concerns. The consumer-is-king mentality renders all established and time-tested practices unstable and utterly negotiable.

The Disappearance of "Human Nature"

Another factor that impacts the possibility of documents such as creeds having any usefulness is the disappearance of "human nature" as a category. This is often not done explicitly, except by the most extreme advocates of postmodern skepticism; but functionally the idea of a human nature or "essence" that connects people in one time and place to another is today often neglected or ignored. Numerous factors play into this. One is that the modern world has made everyone more acutely aware of the vast variety of social and cultural practices exhibited by different groups. The Englishman of the nineteenth century might have been able to rest secure in the knowledge that taking afternoon tea was the way human beings should act and that those who did not do so were either weird (if English), or dastardly (if French, Italian, or German), or inferior (if otherwise foreign). Now, however, we know that afternoon refreshment practices are scarcely the result of the structure of the human genome. More seriously, we know that practices considered disgusting by one group, such as female circumcision, are yet considered necessary by others. This raises the question of whether there are universal human values and rights and, if so, what criteria are to be used to determine what they are. If eating pork is unacceptable to Jews, does that mean that French pig farmers should be closed down? What, if anything, is the common cultural, ethical, philosophical, or metaphysical core that binds human beings together? Indeed, does such a thing exist?

If "human nature" does not exist, other than as a specific, basic biological structure that means one human can only reproduce in conjunction with another, then what authority can anybody or any human document that belongs to another time or place have? If human nature is really a construct of the particulars of a specific historical, geographical, and cultural context, it is not immediately obvious that, say, a document produced in Constantinople near the end of the fourth century can have any relevance to people living in London or New York at the start of the twenty-first. For historical documents to speak beyond their own time there has to be some kind of fundamental continuity between their form and content and the present age.

Consumerism plays its part here as well. If you are what you consume, if you can be whatever you want to be, then what binds you to your neighbor? More importantly, what binds you to the people in other times and places? If you are master of your own destiny, then you are free to act toward the past and toward other people in the same way you act toward the goods on the supermarket shelf. You buy what appeals to you and leave behind that which does not.

The implications for creeds and confessions are obvious. Choose your particular: they were written by dead, white males who dressed differently to us, had different attitudes to the world, spoke in a different language, were celibate, were not celibate, never understood technology or listened to Elvis, never grappled with the scientific breakthroughs of recent years, etc., etc. If nothing binds us to them, or if the differences between us and them simply overwhelm any analogy there might be between us, then they have nothing useful or relevant to say to us, and we are better off ignoring them. A world in which human nature is merely a construct put together by the individual or by the specific community in which the individual is placed is a world where historical documents, such as creeds, can have no transcendent significance but are doomed to be of merely local or antiquarian interest.

Words, Mysticism, and Pragmatism

If devaluing the past is one aspect of contemporary culture that militates against the usefulness of creeds and confessions, a second is the current suspicion of words as reliable means of communication.

We need to acknowledge at the outset that there is plenty of evidence for the problematic nature of words. To quote The Police: "Poets, priests and politicians have words to thank for their positions."[1] The idea that words are one way to establish and maintain personal power and prestige is deeply rooted. Indeed, a whole school of literary theory has developed around this notion, whereby words have become little more than tools to be used to marginalize and manipulate others. I remember some years ago watching a 1930s Nazi propaganda film entitled *Sein ohne Leben* ("Being without Life"), which was designed to make the case that children born with severe mental and physical disabilities should be euthanized. The documentary was significant in that it helped pave the way for the social and cultural context in which the broader policies of the Holocaust could be pursued. But what interested me in particular was the way it used those two words—"being" and "life"—as a means of making a manipulative distinction that served to obscure the horror of what was really being proposed. By implying that a child with severe encephalitis possessed a mere existence and no life, by driving that wedge between the two, the child was effectively and quietly robbed of personhood and thus of status. The words were not being used to convey information; they were being used to create a reality and one that, in the wake of the Holocaust, looks vile and manipulative.

One could add to this many examples drawn from the sphere of politics, perhaps the most notorious realm for such linguistic twisting. In short, the case for words being susceptible to manipulative usage is not one that can be credibly questioned. Such has led to a broader cultural cynicism about language, which has bled over into the church. That Christianity is a way of life and not a set of propositions has become something of a mantra among younger Christians in the last ten years. Of course, like most erroneous notions, it contains just enough truth and has just enough legitimate criticism of alternative positions to be credible. Indeed, one of its underlying concerns—that Christianity not terminate in a mere intellectualism—is surely legitimate, even if the sweeping terms in which this is expressed clearly involve an unbiblical reduction of Christianity to praxis. It is not actually that original: Desiderius Erasmus, Richard Baxter, and Adolf von Har-

---

[1] The Police, "De Do Do Do, De Da Da Da," *Zenyattà Mondatta*, December 5, 1980.

nack, to name but three, all offered variations (of differing degrees of orthodoxy) on this theme. Yet the frequency with which it occurs in the history of the church indicates that at least some of the concerns it seeks to address must be legitimate.

In addition to the obvious problems with the way language has been used by people such as politicians, and how sophisticated literary theorists have dismantled old linguistic certainties, there is also a popular strain of mysticism (for want of a better word) that pervades modern culture and that is profoundly suspicious of words. This takes various forms. One thinks, for example, of the notion that certain emotional sentiments or responses constitute truth, something that is often epitomized by the kind of statements made with remarkable regularity on TV talk shows. "I just know in my heart that it is true" is built on this kind of thinking. Many of us no doubt have encountered ethical argumentation that amounts to, or perhaps is even expressed as, "It feels so good. How can it possibly be wrong?"[2]

Again, we might turn to popular music to provide a summary of this kind of thinking. If the reader will forgive the obvious incoherence of using words to undermine confidence in words, here are a few lines from Madonna's song, "Bedtime Stories":

> Words are useless, especially sentences.
> They don't stand for anything.
> How could they explain how I feel?

Madonna actually makes quite a profound point here: the modern emphasis on emotions as the locus of truth or, to use the trendier term, authenticity, is fundamentally non- and even antiverbal. When someone declares that they "just know in their heart" that the latest boy band is the greatest phenomenon of Western musical culture since Bach left the organ loft for the last time, you may know that they are talking arrant nonsense, but there is no way that you can refute this person's claim because it is not a claim expressed using public criteria

---

[2]For all of the plausibility of such emotive arguments in modern culture when it comes to, say, teenagers sleeping together, we still live in an age when thankfully this is not yet considered a plausible justification for serial killers.

commonly known as words and logic. It is a purely personal, subjective judgment; and, in its claim to truth, it makes truth something mystical, something to be experienced, not something subject to normal criteria of public evaluation.

To have such an attitude so deeply embedded in popular culture, whether pop songs or talk shows or the visceral level of public discourse one often witnesses on the television in scenes outside courthouses, political rallies, and sporting events, would in itself create plenty of difficulties for the notion of creeds and confessions. Yet we see the impact of suspicion of words even within the Christian church. At the Reformation, preaching came to supplant the Mass as the central act of corporate Christian worship; underlying this shift was a move toward an understanding of the gospel as promise and of salvation as being by faith in that promise. Thus, proclamation of that promise in words moved to center stage. In recent decades, however, many churches have shifted preaching from this central place. In some contexts, preaching has not been abandoned; rather, it has been relativized and now stands alongside dramatic performances, candles, incense, and small group discussion. In other contexts, preaching has been pushed completely aside for conversational discourse, where the authoritative voice of the preacher has been replaced by a more democratic dialogue. Underlying all these shifts, in practice if not always in terms of self-conscious planning, is a suspicion that proclaimed words are no longer a reliable authority or, perhaps better, a *plausible* authority, given the wider antiverbal cultural dispositions.

Populist suspicion of words is not the only point at which the antiverbal mystical emphasis bites the church. Such also has deep and highly sophisticated roots within the history of modern theology. For example, this kind of mysticism is analogous to the kind of revision of the notion of Christian theology that took place at the hands of F. D. E. Schleiermacher, the so-called Father of Liberalism, at the start of the nineteenth century. In the wake of the Enlightenment, and particularly in response to Immanuel Kant's critique of traditional epistemologies, Schleiermacher sought to rebuild the Christian faith in a manner that would be plausible in his context. As the notions of objective truth and of the possibility of generalizing universal truths from the particulars of history had been abandoned, Schleiermacher offered an account of Christian theology which understood doctrine not so much as statements about the nature of God as a description of religious psychology. Thus, for example, predestination ceased to be what it appeared on paper to be—a statement about God's eternal purpose relative to men and women—and became rather a poetic expression of the feeling of total dependence upon God as experienced by the religious individual. Further, Christ became supremely important as the incarnation of God not because he was the incarnate God in the traditional manner defined by the Chalcedonian Definition of 451, but rather because in him the consciousness of God was supremely manifested.

Within such a framework, then, propositional, doctrinal Christianity (and the creeds and confessions that epitomized it) was exchanged for something mystical and experiential. Of course, to tar this with the label "liberalism" is likely to precipitate an immediate reaction from self-styled conservative evangelicals. Liberalism is the enemy; it is what "they" hold to—whoever "they" are—and not something of which we are guilty ourselves. Yet mysticism is alive and well within evangelical circles. Anyone who has ever been told by a friend that the Lord led such a friend to do something completely silly, or anyone who has ever been at a Bible study where the burden has been to explain "what the text means to me," regardless of what the words on the page and the grammar and syntax might otherwise indicate, has experienced an evangelical mysticism that is not really distinguishable from traditional liberalism at the level of its understanding of what constitutes truth.

Closely allied to mysticism is another phenomenon lethal to confessional Christianity: pragmatism, the notion that truth is to be found in usefulness. When one reflects for a moment on talk-show style mysticism, this becomes obvious. When individuals on such shows declare that "I just know in my heart that this is true," what they are often saying is, "This belief works for me; it has some actual, practical result that I like." Whether the belief makes them more cheerful, or helps them to feel more important, or gives them hope for better times ahead, the important thing is not so much the content of the belief as its result.

Such thinking pervades much of modern church life. I noted above the student in class who questioned the usefulness of creeds and confessions today. By her application of such a category to the creeds, she immediately indicated the pragmatic tendency of her thinking. We might also reflect upon the pragmatic content of so many books written by and for evangelical Christians. Here, for example, is the Amazon blurb for *The Eden Diet: A Biblical and Merciful Weight Loss Program*:

> The Eden Diet helps readers understand the many reasons why they have not been able to lose weight in the past. In most cases, they fail to eat according to their God-given internal sensations—their hunger pangs. Hunger was meant to be a compass that tells people when and how much to eat. However, most overweight people eat for external reasons that have little to do with hunger. They eat according to the clock, because of automatic habits, in response to their emotions and fleshly desires, or in response to tantalizing advertising messages. The Eden Diet shows how to overcome those fattening habits. It explains how to eat in response to the body's internal signals, how to block out external stimuli that trigger eating, and how to lose weight and achieve the abundant life God intended for His children in the beginning. Specific advice is given that helps readers eat for weight loss at pot luck events, buffets, at restaurants, on holidays and special occasions, and any time they are faced with challenging emotions and sinful desires.[3]

This book is available as an audio download from a well-known evangelical publisher, a publisher that lists on its website, as of July 2011, a large number of Christian diet books, including *Fit for My King: His Princess Diet Plan and Devotional*; *The Maker's Diet: The 40-Day Health Experience That Will Change Your Life Forever*; the two-volume *Never Say Diet Personal Fitness Trainer*; and the intriguing but presumably overstated *New Bible Cure for Cancer*.

---

[3] Amazon.com book description of Rita M. Hancock's *The Eden Diet: A Biblical and Merciful Christian Weight Loss Program* (Oklahoma City: Personalized Fitness Products, 2008), http://www.amazon.com/Eden-Diet-Biblical-Merciful-Christian/dp/0982034105/ref= sr_1_1?ie=UTF8&qid=1310558775&sr=8-1.

The existence of such books within Christianity is a study in itself, since it speaks eloquently about a range of topics, from how people understand the essence of Christianity to what they see as the ideal Christian life. For our purpose here, it is sufficient to note the profound pragmatism that these titles indicate: Christianity is all about what it can do for you in the here and now. Similar genres exist within the evangelical world for financial planning, education, and self-fulfillment. All are evidence that the pragmatism of the wider world is alive and well within the walls of the church.

In such a culture, it is not surprising that creeds and confessions do not appear particularly useful. One will search in vain in the creeds of the ancient church for advice on how to stop excessive snacking between meals or on how to avoid a second trip to the dessert table at a potluck lunch. Further, while I cannot claim comprehensive knowledge of every confessional document written during the Reformation, none, as far as I know offer the reader a personal trainer, a wonderful "health experience," financial prosperity, or a cure for cancer. By the standards of the culture that has produced the Eden diet, one would have to say that the confessional heritage of the church is really rather useless.

Finally, remember that the comment about the irrelevance of creeds and confessions was made by a student who was a member of a confessional church in one of my classes at a confessional seminary. It is not only the less doctrinally informed areas of evangelicalism that have been impacted by the priorities of Oprah and company. Ask yourself this: if my church put on a conference about how to have a great Christian marriage and fulfilled sex life, would more or fewer people attend than if we did one on the importance of the incarnation or the Trinity? The answer to that question allows an interesting comparison between the priorities of the church today and that of the fourth and fifth centuries. It is not that the people in your church do not believe that, say, Christ rose from the dead and the tomb was empty; rather it is that such belief has no real usefulness to them other than as it provides them with what they are looking to obtain in the here and now. In such a context, orthodoxy as expressed in the great creeds and confessions is not rejected; it is simply sidelined as irrelevant and essentially useless.

Antiauthoritarianism

If there are deep forces within our culture that militate against creeds and confessions on the basis of their nature as historical and linguistic documents, there are also forces that strike deep at these documents in terms of their origin and their status. Creeds and confessions are, by definition, statements made by institutions (churches), and they derive their practical authority from their connection to such institutions. It is true that some confessions have a single author. The Belgic Confession, written by the French Protestant Guido de Bres, is one obvious example; but it possesses its authority because it has been adopted by a church as an authoritative document. In the case of the Belgic Confession, this adoptive action was taken by the Synod of Dordt, which met in 1618–1619 in the city of Dordrecht in the Netherlands. It is the sanction of a corporate body that gives the confession its legal ecclesiastical status, not the specific identity of the author.

This institutional aspect of creeds and confessions is culturally problematic. Indeed, if anything marks the contemporary world it is surely suspicion of external authority. One might generalize and say that the issues noted above, with science, technology, consumerism, language, mysticism, and pragmatism, are all variations on the theme of rejection of external authority, that of the past in the case of science and technology, and that of anything but the self in terms of consumerism, language, and the rest.

Of course, this rejection of external authority is ultimately rather selective. While many today reject traditional forms of external authority (family hierarchies, civil governments, traditional moral values, etc.), those same people often accept rather uncritically other forms of external authority. Think, for example, of the mindless emulation of the fashions of pop stars by their fans; or the incredibly naïve confidence that is often placed in the opinions of vacuous and ill-informed celebrities on, say, third world debt or global warming, as opposed to those of traditional experts. Youth culture is the same: why on earth would anyone want the opinion of the latest boy band on anything unless he was convinced that knowledge gained by experience, knowledge from "out there," was actually a hindrance to truth and not a means of accessing it? Yet the blogs and the news media crave the views of the likes of Lady Gaga on all kinds of things of which they are technically ignorant and actually incapable of expressing themselves with any coherence or thoughtfulness. They are authorities not because of their knowledge or skills but because of their status in our modern consumer society; and the fact that they are relatively young (or like to think that they are, as in the case of the superannuated Bono) is strangely seen as a plus, an advantage, something that qualifies them to make these statements. As I noted above, it is hard to imagine applying the same criteria to, say, electricians or brain surgeons, where age and experience are typically seen as essential qualifications. Strange to tell, on the bigger questions and problems of the world and society, having "relevant training and knowledge" is more likely to earn one excoriation as "an ivory tower academic" or part of the dreaded "establishment" than a useful contributor to any proposed solution. Lady Gaga is apparently more likely to have the answer to human sexuality or third world debt than a minister or an economist. Arguably, therefore, the rejection of external authority needs to be carefully defined as the rejection of *traditional forms* of external authority in order to be an accurate statement.

Even with this qualification, however, the church—or at least the traditional church, with its structures of governance, its established ways of doing things, and its creeds and confessions—fares badly. Ironically, the old forms of authority have been replaced by new ones; self-appointed gurus abound, as do theological and antitheological potboilers. But my concern is not with passing fads; it is with a recovering of traditional and, as I will argue, biblical patterns of institutional authority.

First, however, it is worth spending a few moments examining why respect for traditional external authority is at such a pitiable state today. It is clear that the same forces that made consumerism an antihistorical force also militate against traditional institutional authority. Consumerism is built upon the notion of the construction of self-identity through consumption. Fashions in clothing are a great example of this. Whether it is the shirt of one's favorite sports team or a style of dress adopted by one's favorite TV or pop star, at the heart of fashion is the notion that by purchasing certain goods one can create an identity for oneself.

Broadening out from fashion, the world of commercial advertising is predicated on this kind of self-creating consumption. Commercials are not simply designed to create dissatisfaction with the present and thus to orient the audience toward the future; they are also designed to send the signal that you can make yourself different, you can become the ideal person you wish to be, by purchasing some particular goods or services. This is not simply a matter of creating needs; it is also about sending a message that you are master of your own universe. The Nike sales pitch, "Just do it!" might as easily be written "Just be it!" for, with a credit card in your pocket, you can become whatever you want to be. Authority lies within you, or at least that is the message the sales and marketing people wish to send; external authority is merely a repressive force that prevents you from being whoever and whatever you wish to be.

We also see a kind of mysticism and pragmatism in anti-authoritarianism, where the locus of authority is ultimately not an external institution or body of knowledge but rather the inner being of the person. If "it" is "true for me" because "I just know it in my heart," then guess what? "My heart," whether that is a feeling of happiness or of self-esteem or of whatever, is the authority: internal, mystical, appointed by me using pragmatic criteria and as far away from any notion of direct external or institutional authority as is possible. Of course, it does not take a genius to realize that so many of the things that we "just know in our hearts" do actually come from external authorities—commercials, idiotic talk shows, television pundits—but that is not the point. The point is that we do not consciously understand this or recognize such authorities as having that effect.

One further factor that militates against traditional notions of external institutional authority is the Internet, specifically the world of blogs and tweets. There are, of course, different types of blogs. I myself do a bit of blogging for an e-zine, *reformation21*. For me, it is simply an electronic form of traditional journalism. I write articles, and the editor publishes them. One thing that *reformation21* does not do is allow "comments" to be made by random readers on the content. Anyone can write to the editor; and, in the current virtual world, it takes very little effort to track down an author's e-mail and send one's thoughts straight to the source. But the deregulated posting of public comments is not allowed.

From my perspective, this is a good thing. I have yet to read a "comments thread" on any topic of significance that does not quickly degenerate into moronic commentary that is as notable for its vacuousness as it is for its personal abuse. The culture of the comments thread is one which has confused the right to speak with the right to be heard and which sends a rather uncritical signal to the world about what constitutes good argumentation and appropriate contributions to discussion. Yet the visceral reaction with which such "comment free" e-zines meet from some individuals speaks once again of a culture where an anarchic free-for-all apparently is the only acceptable way of approaching a topic. The democratization of discussion in this way is inimical to traditional notions of authority and to the traditional notions of knowledge and expertise which underlie them. Again, we might note that this is a selective repudiation of authority: I have never read a comments thread on a blog dealing with brain surgery or rocket science, but I doubt that the good ones in these fields contain too many comments about "Nazis" or end with remarks like "Fantastic stuff guys !!! ☺" by people signing themselves off as "Crazydogguy" and the like. Politics and theology are much more likely to attract such discourse, it seems, and this surely indicates, and reinforces, the wider cultural problem with the kind of authority associated with traditional institutions when it comes to what we might term the more philosophical aspects of life.

Of course, it is not just the anarchy of the blogs that plays to this kind of attitude. The arrival of Wikipedia and the like is also significant. Now, I confess that I am something of a Wikipedia fan. It is a fantastic resource for finding out the ages of favorite movie stars and the kind of trivia on a variety of subjects that is most useful when one is taking part in a pub quiz. The problem is that it can give the impression that a subject can be mastered in a very short period of time. I remember a few years ago reading a blog where a person was telling the world that he had never heard of presuppositional apologetics until that morning, had read the Wikipedia article on the same, and that it had completely changed his life. Indeed, he may even have specified the time—11:23

a.m. comes to mind—at which this earth-shattering change took place. The point was ridiculous: whether presuppositional apologetics is capable of such impact is one question, but that a Wikipedia article could provide sufficient information to achieve this is surely unlikely. Were it so, then one could only conclude that all those who reject the position are either mad, stupid, or have never read the article. A most unlikely scenario, methinks.

What these things—anarchic blog comments, the assumption that reading a Wikipedia article gives true insight—witness to is the creation of a culture of knowledge in which little weight is placed upon expertise and the idea that competence in some things only comes after extended periods of hard work and training. They are thus further factors in the complex of cultural forces that discount traditional sources of authority—institutions, traditions, etc.—and replace them with sources that derive their authority from something else, not least the hip trendiness of the latest fad or celebrity.

It seems clear to me that this anti-institutional tendency is deep-rooted even within churches that, on paper, place a premium on structure and authority. For example, in my own denomination, the Orthodox Presbyterian Church (OPC), we have a book of church order that lays out the basic structures of the church and the procedures by which these are to be maintained. Office-bearers (ministers, elders, deacons) take strict vows that bind them to particular doctrinal positions (the Westminster Standards) but also to the denomination and the local congregation. All the office-bearers with whom I have been privileged to serve over the years have taken their vows very seriously.

What is less often noted, however, is that members, too, take vows. In the OPC these vows are not the same as those of office-bearers. This is for good reason; the qualifications for office bearing, as opposed to being a member, are somewhat more stringent, as we shall explore in a later chapter. But while the content of the vows for members may be less stringent in terms of specifics, they are no less serious in terms of their binding quality. In the OPC they involve profession of faith in the Trinity, trust in Christ for salvation, and commitment to the local body and submission under God—a key qualification—to the elders.

What never ceases to amaze me is the casual way in which people make and break membership vows, sometimes within weeks. I have seen individuals leave the church because they were not given the Sunday school teaching opportunities they thought they deserved, because they did not like the worship style, and because their children found a more interesting church elsewhere. That such reasons do not give any grounds for breaking vows never seems to register. Indeed, some leave without giving any reason at all, so lightly do they regard solemn vows taken before God and the church.

Now, I would never advocate that someone cannot leave a church at which they are very unhappy; and thankfully, there is provision for people to be able to move if they decide to. Cults take away people's freedom; the church should never do that. But there are processes by which this can be done, typically through discussion with the elders, which actually seek to honor the integrity of the vows. What is striking is that these processes are, in my experience, rarely used as they should be. Often the first thing that the elders hear is that somebody has already left and would like a letter of transfer to his new church or simply to be erased from the membership rolls.

What this phenomenon tells me is that the suspicion of, or (perhaps better) indifference to, the external authority of institutions is as deeply embedded in the culture of the contemporary church as it is in society. And such an attitude inevitably has an impact on the way creeds and confessions are viewed. The person who has no real, practical respect for the church as an institution is inevitably going to have little respect for the documents that church has produced and/or authorized as part of the basic means by which she identifies herself, witnesses to the world, and maintains some level of order within her ranks.

The Fear of Exclusion

One further cultural proclivity worth mentioning is that of the fear of exclusion, of drawing boundaries such that some people belong and other people do not. In addressing this matter, it is important to note that much of the tragedy of human history, particularly more recent history, has been wrapped up with the problem of exclusion. One need only think of the Armenian genocide of 1915, the Holocaust, the Rape of Nanking, the Balkan crisis, and the gassing of the Kurds to understand how vicious some forms of exclusion can be. Racism is only the most obvious; we can all think of other, less obvious, forms of exclusion that also help to justify crimes, great and small, perpetrated by one group of human beings against others.

Such forms of exclusion have left many with a lasting fear of anything that might smack of looking down on others as inferior. In the silly extremes of political correctness, it almost seems that anything at which I choose to take offense is to be deemed oppressive, exclusionary, and on the slippery slope to some form of genocide or holocaust. Yet we must not allow the excesses of the PC types to blind us to the really genuine concerns that underlie this fear of exclusion; but nor must we be blind to the impact it has upon attitudes to things like statements of faith and confessions.

A confession is a positive statement of belief; but in making a positive statement of belief, it inevitably excludes those who disagree with its content. Even the most tenuous confessions do this: the Unitarian may claim a creedless faith, but he is never going to invite a Trinitarian, who insists upon the nonnegotiability of the Trinity, to fill his pulpit; Trinitarians are therefore excluded. And if it is true that the creedless faith of the Unitarian inevitably excludes some, how much more true is this of orthodox Christian creeds and confessions? The Athanasian Creed is the most spectacular of these as it contains not only positive statement of Christian doctrine but also anathemas against those who disagree with its teaching. It is explicitly, not merely implicitly, an instrument of exclusion.

Trajectories of thought that take their cue from traditional Christian liberalism have little or no patience with such exclusivism, of course, because they see doctrinal statements not as transcendent truth claims but as expressions of the religious psychology of the individual or the particular religious community. Whether the inspiration for this is the kind of Kantian theology of Schleiermacher or the linguistic philosophy of Wittgenstein, the net result is the same: the truth claims of one community do not apply in any real or straightforward way to another; thus the problem of excluding some is localized and limited.

This is my truth; tell me yours (to quote the title of the Manic Street Preachers' 1998 album).

The last decade has intensified this fear of exclusion particularly when it comes to religion. The impact of religiously motivated or religiously expressed terrorism such as the attack on American institutions on September 11, 2001, has created a cultural atmosphere scarcely conducive to exclusive religious truth claims. One can see this in various responses that have been offered to the rise of alleged religious radicalism. There is the increasingly commonplace use of the catch-all term "fundamentalism" and its cognates that presumably lumps anyone who takes their religion seriously together under the same scary category, the wild-eyed Jihadist suicide bomber and the aged Amish grandmother. That fundamentalism equals violence is virtually a given for many.

Reaction within the religious world to this cultural moment is interesting. Within Christian circles, the decade after 9/11 saw the rise and fall of the cluster of movements grouped together as the emergent church, with its emphasis on Christianity as a way of life, not a set of doctrines, and its prioritizing of belonging before believing. This latter slogan, of course, can only make sense if belonging and believing are actually separable in a more than merely formal way. Such a notion is, in the case of many emergent leaders, built on assumed postmodern epistemologies. These are themselves in origin connected to the rise of postcolonialism, with its fear of the hegemony of the white man's religion and the imperialist use of Western ideologies, of which Christianity is perhaps the most obvious and historically influential.

This fear has meant that a Christianity that is committed to truth claims which apply beyond the community of faith or which exclude certain people from that community is profoundly at odds with the cultural current. Strange to tell, we do still live in societies that routinely exclude people. The fact that prisons are full to bursting indicates that society still considers some forms of behavior to be unacceptable and demands their exclusion from mainstream social life. Legislation against discrimination on the basis of race, creed, or sexual orientation indicates that some views are beyond the pale, and those who hold them are not to express them in practical terms in the public sphere. Yet religion, particularly traditional religion, finds itself at a cultural moment where it is feared because it dares to say that some beliefs and practices are true and good while others are false and bad. Such a moment is scarcely conducive to any form of creedalism or confessionalism.

One further, and perhaps unusual, example of this fear of exclusion is the phenomenon known as evangelicalism, typically understood as a conservative, orthodox form of Protestantism marked by an emphasis on conversion and evangelism. Evangelicalism is a somewhat balkanized phenomenon, and its various tribes, or subtribes, often have little difficulty in drawing lines that exclude others who regard themselves as evangelicals from their own particular group. Nevertheless, what evangelicalism in all of its forms typically does is prioritize parachurch institutions over and above the church. Whether we are talking in the United States of the National Association of Evangelicals or The Gospel Coalition, or in Britain of the Evangelical Alliance or Affinity, we are talking about coalition movements, and coalition movements by their very definition require broad statements of faith.

These groups all have statements of faith; but they are statements of faith designed to keep in the tent all the various sects of which the clan chiefs approve. Thus, matters that are vital to the constitution of actual churches (a clear position on baptism, for example) are typically left to one side, on the grounds that the parachurch leaders do not wish to exclude people because of such matters. The statements are therefore often brief and, compared to, say, the Belgic Confession or the Westminster, highly attenuated.

This is not necessarily a problem, provided that nobody forgets that these groups are not churches and that they are therefore always to be subordinate to churches in the way Christians think about the practical outworking of their faith. Too often, however, the impression is given that these groups, representing this nebulous phenomenon "evangelicalism," consider themselves to be the higher synthesis and the context where the real action takes place. The culture that such an attitude reflects ultimately tends to send the message to Christians that issues such as baptism are of minor importance, and that the matters which divide denominations are trivial and even sinful in the way they keep Presbyterians and Baptists from belonging to the same church. This is, ironically, not a million miles from the wider culture's fear of exclusion and actually sets such professedly conservative evangelicals on an odd continuum with many of the emergents whom they would repudiate. The difference between the conservative evangelical and the emergent might be profound at the level of epistemology, but in terms of regarding doctrine as negotiable and traditional structures of church authority as practically irrelevant, the difference might not be as great as is often imagined.

Conclusion: Creeds, Confessions, and Distasteful Christianity

In outlining various cultural factors that militate against the use of creeds and confessions in the church, I am not arguing that every minister or every believer who declares they have "no creed but the Bible" is necessarily in thrall to all or any of the above. Indeed, some of the most militant "no creed" people I have ever come across have been very much on the hardline separatist wing of the Christian church and scarcely vulnerable to accusations that they are capitulating to the wider cultural fear of excluding someone. They have a legitimate fear that creeds and confessions can end up in certain circumstances supplanting Scripture and becoming the sole authority in the way the church operates.

What we have seen, however, is that there are powerful currents within modern life that militate in various ways against the positive use of creeds and confessions in the church. These currents often go unnoticed by those of us who have no choice but to live, move, and have our being within them. Thus, the pastor who thinks he is being biblical by declaring he has no creed but the Bible may actually, upon reflection, find that his position is more shaped by the modern world than he at first realized. Rather than instinctively taking his cue from the historic practices of the church, he may in fact really be shaped by the wider world. The stories the modern world tells us are powerful: the future-oriented promise of science, the technology that privileges the young, the materialistic paradise offered by consumerism, which is always just around the next corner, the dying of confidence in words, the fragmentation of human nature, the distrust of traditional structures and notions of authority, and the wicked results of saying that somebody else is wrong and does not belong. All of these in their different ways make the idea of doctrinal Christianity, expressed in creeds and confessions, both implausible and distasteful; and all of them are part of the cultural air we all breathe.

This leads to a very important distinction. Modern culture has not really rendered creeds and confessions untrue; far less has it rendered them unbiblical. But it has rendered them implausible and distasteful. They are implausible because they are built on old-fashioned notions of truth and language. They make the claim that a linguistic formulation of a state of affairs can have a binding authority beyond the mere text on the page, that creeds actually refer to something, and that that something has a significance for all of humanity. They thus demand that individuals submit, intellectually and morally, to something outside of themselves, that they listen to the voices from the church from other times and other places. They go directly against the grain of an antihistorical, antiauthoritarian age. Creeds strike hard at the cherished notion of human autonomy and of the notion that I am exceptional, that the normal rules do not apply to me in the way they do to others.

They are distasteful for the same reason: because they make old-fashioned truth claims; and to claim that one position is true is automatically to claim that its opposite is false. God cannot exist and not exist at the same time; he cannot be three persons and one person at the same time, at least not without unhelpful and hopeless equivocation (despite the claims of some Reformed theologians to the contrary). Truth claims thus imply a hierarchy whereby one position is better than another and where some beliefs, and thus those who hold those beliefs, are excluded. That may not be a very tasteful option in today's society but, as noted above, even the modern pluralist West still excludes those that it considers, if not wrong, then at least distasteful and unpleasant.

We are naïve as Christians if we think that our thinking is not shaped by the cultural currents that surround us. Of course, we cannot abstract ourselves from our context; we cannot cease to be embodied individuals, each with our own personal biographies, who live within a complex network of social relations that influence the way we live and think and speak. Yet to know something of our context is to make ourselves aware of some of the invisible forces that have such an unconscious influence on us. Once we know they are there, we at least have the possibility of engaging in critical reflection, which will allow us to some extent to liberate ourselves from them—or, if not to liberate ourselves, at least to make us more aware of why we think the way we do.

Thus, I conclude this chapter by posing a challenge to those who, in their earnest desire to be faithful to Scripture as the supreme authority of faith and life, claim that they have no creed but the Bible. Reflect critically on the cultural forces that are certainly consonant with holding such a position and ask yourself whether they have perhaps reinforced your antipathy to creeds and confessions in a way that is not directly related to the Bible's own teaching at all. Then, setting aside for just a moment your sincere convictions on this matter, read the rest of this book and see whether creeds and confessions might not actually provide you with a better way of preserving precisely those aspects of biblical, Christian faith which are most valuable to you and which you passionately wish to communicate to your church.

2

The Foundations of Creedalism

The cultural currents that make creedalism implausible in the current climate are powerful and often so pervasive as to be virtually invisible. This was the basic burden of chapter 1; and those are very naïve who think that the church is immune to these currents when it comes to how she understands the significance of creeds and confessions. The speciously biblical cry of "No creed but the Bible!" is not as straight-forwardly countercultural as many might think. The next question, of course, is, exactly how biblical is this cry anyway?

In this chapter, I do not intend to refute, point by point, all of the challenges I outlined in chapter 1. Rather I want to focus on a positive exposition of a series of positions that, taken together, will require the church which rejects confessions to realize just how much unbiblical ideas have shaped her thinking in this area and thus to revise her attitude toward creeds and confessions. First, I make a case for the importance and adequacy of words in the biblical narrative and thus our under-standing of God and his revelation. Second, I point to biblical teaching that human beings are not self-created but possess, for want of a better word, an essence that is given to them from without. Third, I point to evidence within the Bible of the use of creed-like statements and the need to transmit "forms of sound words." Finally, I outline New Testament teaching on biblical church government and thus of an institutional church that is charged with faithful transmission of the faith.

The Adequacy of Words

While the problems outlined in chapter 1 are considerable, there are still very good reasons why the church should formulate, adopt, and use creeds and confessions. These reasons are rooted in theological considerations that serve to relativize and weaken the kind of cultural objections we have noted, both those from the wider world and those from the evangelical sphere.

Foundational to this creedal formulation is a biblical understanding of the nature of God himself and fundamental to the biblical idea of God is the fact that he is a God who speaks. We see this in the language used in John 1:

> In the beginning was the Word, and the Word was with God, and the Word was God.

We need to be careful in how literally we take the language of "Word" here, for the Son is not a word spoken by the Father in the way that I might say "automobile" or "classic rock album." I move my vocal chords and vibrate molecules of air at a certain frequency; God does neither relative to the eternal generation of the Son. But John is clearly making an analogy between the Father and the Son and the speaker and the word spoken. Yet the notion of God as being a God characterized by speech does not rest on the prologue of John's Gospel. Right at the very inception of history, the moment when time itself began, the creative activity of God is described in terms of speech:

> In the beginning, God created the heavens and the earth. The earth was without form and void, and darkness was over the face of the deep. And the Spirit of God was hovering over the face of the waters.
> And God said, "Let there be light," and there was light. And God saw that the light was good. And God separated the light from the darkness. (Gen. 1:1–4)

In this passage, the light is created by the word of God's power. Indeed, the very first divine action of which we hear in the Bible is that God speaks. There is nothing; God speaks; and then there is something—and that something is a direct result of the act of divine speech. His word is thus powerful and creative. Indeed, it is definitive of what exists; and, of course, the continuation of Genesis 1 and 2 indicates that this speech is crucial to the further creative acts, culminating in the internal divine conversation which leads directly to the creation of man and woman in the divine image.

The biblical narrative quickly makes it clear that divine speech is to be a fundamental aspect of the special relationship that exists between God and those made in his image. Genesis 1:28–30 establishes the basic status and duties of humanity in relation to the created world, with God speaking to the man and the woman and telling them what they are to do, what authority they have, what they may eat, and what they must not eat. The arrangement is articulated using words; it is linguistic in its basic form.

The importance of language as a means not simply of communication but of defining and sustaining the relationship of God and humanity continues after the fall. God curses the serpent and then tells the woman and the man how their relationship with him, with each other, and with the creation itself is changed as a result of the fall (Gen. 3:14–19). In pronouncing this curse, God is not simply describing what has happened; he is bringing the state of affairs into existence.

The same kind of linguistic action is found in Genesis 15, where God enters into covenant with Abraham, and thus starts the long process of election in history that will culminate in the coming of Jesus Christ and the kingdom of God. Again, words are central, this time not to the creation but to the anticipation of the new creation. The promise, like the curse before it, is not simply a description of a state of affairs; it is constitutive of the state of affairs that it brings into existence between God and Abraham.

As well as being active and creative, God's word, God's speaking, is also a means of his presence. One interesting example of this is provided by the story of Elisha and the Shunammite in 2 Kings 4. The story starts as one of the most delightful in all of Scripture. The

Shunammite is a wealthy lady who decides to build an extra room on the roof of her house so that whenever Elisha passes through her town, he knows that he can have a place to stay. In return for her kindness, Elisha asks his servant to find out from the woman what there is that she lacks which he can provide. So unassuming and selfless is she that she simply responds that she lives among her friends and family and thus has all that she could want; she is so selfless that she does not even think to bring to the prophet's attention her childlessness, a source of social shame as well as (presumably) personal sadness. Nevertheless, the servant notices her lack and reports it to the prophet who then declares that, within a year, she will give birth to a child.

So far, so good. Then, of course, the child grows up, and when he is old enough to be in the fields with his father but still young enough to sit on his mother's knee, he has some kind of seizure, which leads to his death. In a scene of brutal, heart-breaking realism, the woman races to find the man of God and collapses at his feet in a veritable explosion of grief. Elisha immediately sends his servant with his staff to raise the child, but she will not leave the prophet, insisting that he and he alone is the one who must come.

The question is obvious: why? Why this insistence on Elisha? Could his staff not have worked just as effectively, given that God is sovereign and all powerful? The answer lies with the significance of who the prophet is. At that point in Israel's history, the prophet was the one—the only one—through whom the words of God came. We might recast that by saying that he was the only one through whom God was present. Now, of course, there are different modes of divine presence. There is what one might call the bare metaphysical presence of God, which is everywhere and which sustains everything. As God is in Tel Aviv or New York so he is also in Damascus and La Paz. But there is also a presence of God that is active and powerful. Thus, God was present in the ark of the covenant in a way in which he was not present in one of Solomon's wives' jewelry boxes. There were promises attached to his presence in the ark such that the ark was a unique place, which, if touched in a profane or even accidental manner, brought swift retribution to the one who had erred (2 Samuel 6).

Thus, the speech of the prophets was the mode of God's special presence in Israel. That is why the Shunammite needed Elisha and not just his servant and staff. She needed the organ grinder, as we would say in England, and not the monkey. Elisha was the one who not only symbolized God's presence but who, as he—and he alone—spoke God's words, was the very instrument of his presence.

We can infer this further from the way in which the Old Testament can emphasize the *absence* of God. Amos 8 talks of a time when God will turn his back on his people and bring great darkness and despair upon the land. The climactic moment of this description of what we might call "the active absence of God" comes in verses 11–12:

> "Behold, the days are coming," declares the Lord GOD,
>   "when I will send a famine on the land—
> not a famine of bread, nor a thirst for water,
>   but of hearing the words of the LORD.
> They shall wander from sea to sea,
>   and from north to east;
> they shall run to and fro, to seek the word of the LORD,
>   but they shall not find it."

The famine will be of the word of God; and the frantic search of the people for that word is clearly also the frantic search of the people for God himself. His word is not to be found; he himself is absent from his people. That is what will make this moment so terrifying: the silence of God is the absence of God.

This is entirely consistent with what we have noted so far about the function of words in the divine economy of creation and salvation: God's speech is special; it is creative; it defines his relationship to his creation; it defines who his creatures are; it establishes the nature of his special relationship with peoples and individuals; it is the instrument by which he exercises and withdraws his power; and it is perhaps the most significant mode of his presence.

One final biblical note in this context is the baptism of Jesus in Mark 1. In Mark's account, Jesus is baptized, the heavens are torn open, the Spirit descends in the form of a dove, and immediately the Father declares his love for the Son. The language of tearing is significant here. The Greek word *schizein* is used on only one other occasion in Mark's Gospel, at 15:38, where the temple curtain is torn in two. Many readers of the Gospel see this tearing as the opening up of the way for entry in to the Holy of Holies. It is more likely that this represents the outward movement of God from the Holy of Holies. The evidence for this is twofold. The structure of the narrative points clearly in this direction: Jesus dies; the temple curtain is torn in two; and the Gentile centurion who is facing the cross declares that Jesus must have been the Son of God. In other words, the crucifixion is followed by grace flowing to the Gentiles; Mark inserts the curtain incident in-between as a means of underlining this watershed in the history of God's salvific plan.

The second reason for reading the event this way, however, is the connection with Mark 1. When a biblical writer only uses a particular word on two occasions, and both occasions are of obvious significance in the history of salvation, it is reasonable to see if the two can be connected. In fact, the connection lies in the notion of the presence of God. There was apparently an intertestamental Jewish tradition regarding Isaiah 64:1, "Oh that you would rend the heavens and come down, that the mountains might quake at your presence." This tradition saw the rending of the heavens as the eschatological sign that would mark the return of God's Spirit after a long period of absence, the kind of absence described in Amos 8. Thus, Mark's word choice here is very deliberate. Indeed, the strong *schizein* should not be translated as "opened"; if it were so, then Mark 15:38 should presumably be translated in the same way; but "the curtain in the Temple was opened" would obviously be a thoroughly inadequate rendering! In fact, what Mark is doing is signaling to his readers that God's Spirit is about to return, that God is once more going to be present, and, amazing to tell, that is what God immediately does in the very next verse (Mark 1:11). God is once again speaking; he is once again present with his people.[1]

Before we move to the next point, one further comment on God as speaking is important: idols are silent. Psalm 115 makes this point

---

[1]See the discussion of the intertestamental tradition connecting Mark 1:10 to Isaiah 64:1 in James R. Edwards, *The Gospel According to Mark* (Leicester, UK: InterVarsity Press, 2002), 35.

rather dramatically as the psalmist describes the manufactured images of the pagan gods. They have all the attributes of real people—hands, eyes, ears, noses; but none of these things actually functions. They look like the real things, but they are merely impotent fakes. Among all of these, the final one is perhaps the most dramatic: "they do not make a sound in their throat" (v. 7). They are silent, in stark contrast to the God who speaks. Whatever else the true God is, he is not one of the silent gods, for they are the false gods, the idols, the products of the heart of mortals.

There are many theological implications of the identification of God's speech as a special mode of his presence, but the point I want to make here is simple: words are the means God has chosen for his presence and therefore are by definition an adequate means for that presence. Yes, we must accept the reality of all of the suspicion of language that we find in contemporary society, whether of the sophisticated kind exemplified by certain streams of critical theory and literary criticism or the more popular kind found in the mysticism of a Madonna lyric or the supercilious cynicism of the tabloid press. Yet we must also understand that words in themselves are essential elements of our understanding of who God is and quite adequate for theological purposes, even if they can be horribly abused by the humans in the way they use them. They are in fact one of God's chosen means for revealing himself to his people, being present among them, and performing his great saving acts.

Words in Service of the Divine

This divine use of words flows over into the human use of words at a theological level. If words are God's way of being present with his people and working among them, words are also the human means of responding to God and of communicating with each other about God. Again, the Bible itself bears abundant testimony to this fact. Take, for example, the book of Deuteronomy, perhaps the greatest sermon ever preached. Yes, it is part of a divinely inspired canon, but it is also the words of a human being, aimed at other human beings. He speaks God's words to people but in those same words speaks about God. The speech that is Deuteronomy is nothing less than a grand articulation and renewal of the covenant between God and his people, as well as the culminating sermon of Moses's own distinguished career as prophet and preacher.

Yet the use of words for divine, covenant purposes is not restricted to the great and the good in Israel. An example of this is provided in the stipulations surrounding the annual recapitulation of the Passover, which we find in Exodus 12. Having outlined what the children of Israel are to do in the Passover ceremony, Moses speaks of a time when, in future years, the actions will be performed in front of a generation that has no firsthand recollection of what happened on that terrifying night in Egypt:

> And when your children say to you, "What do you mean by this service?" you shall say, "It is the sacrifice of the LORD's Passover, for he passed over the houses of the people of Israel in Egypt, when he struck the Egyptians but spared our houses." (Ex. 12:26–27)

A number of comments are worth making here. First, the importance of history is obvious. The ritual of the Passover is meaningless without the historical framework in which to understand it. If part of the rejection of confessionalism can be seen to lie in the rejection of the importance of history, then it is obvious that such is impossible to square with the Bible. A significant portion of the Bible is historical narrative, and much of what is not yet depends upon that historical narrative for its meaning.

Second, the ritual in and of itself is inadequate for achieving God's purpose, namely, the recollection of God's act of judgment and deliverance in Egypt. It was not enough for the parents merely to repeat the ritual if their children did not understand its significance the first time they saw it. Simply going through the motions again and again would not achieve anything. They needed to explain it to them by the use of words and in a manner that connected the ritual to the events of long ago. It is a simple observation, but this surely indicates both the adequacy of words for communicating important theological truth and their priority over ritual action. This is a point that is made repeatedly throughout the Bible: the prophets often engage in odd theatrics before the people and then explain the meaning of their actions; and Christ himself performs acts that require explanation, whether healings, miraculous feeding, or the Lord's Supper. Words have a special place in the history of God's people as the means of recalling his actions in history and thus of pointing to who he is.

This centrality of words is clear in the ministries of all of the Old Testament prophets. For example, when Isaiah is commissioned in Isaiah 6, he is told specifically to go and *speak* to the people, just as Moses had been told earlier to go and *speak* to Pharaoh. Indeed, what was the role of the prophet if it was not to bring God's judgment and God's promise to bear on the world in general and his people in particular through the medium of words, words proclaiming the identity and the will of God? It is hard to see how judgment or salvation could be proclaimed to people without the use of words. Somehow a simple mime or a liturgical dance would seem rather inadequate to the task. The reason for this is obvious: as God is a speaking God, and human beings are made in his image, so the principle means by which God and humanity relate is that of words.

The role of prophetic preaching continues into the New Testament and, through the paradigmatic significance of the ministries of the apostles and their successors, into the postapostolic world. Paul's polemic against the superapostles in 1 Corinthians is in part an assertion of the power and importance of words in and of themselves. In Corinth, Paul's reputation has suffered because he lacks the aesthetic appeal of the local orators who were by all accounts impressive in both their speaking style and in their physical appearance. In this context, Paul points away from the outward aesthetics of the contemporary orators and to the content of what is said. Preaching is powerful because of the message it communicates (1 Cor. 1:21). The point here is primarily about the message of the gospel, not the form; but the form is surely still important. This is a message that is *preached*; there is no hint that the aesthetic problem should be avoided by the obvious move of simply finding some nonverbal means of communicating the message of the cross. No. The words are still important. Words are not simply adequate for the divine purpose in preaching; they are the divinely sanctioned means of achieving that purpose.

The basic reason for this is that which is clear in the Passover instructions in Exodus 12: God's saving actions are historical, but they need to be interpreted, to be explained by words, in order for the audience to grasp them. The meaning of God's salvation in the Passover is not to be found in some mystical experience of the individual or the community performing the action; rather it is that to which the action refers or that which it signifies, and that can only be explained using words.

The same is true in 1 Corinthians 1. Here Paul emphasizes the cross as the great dividing line that runs through humanity: how one responds to the cross will determine whether one is being saved or one is perishing. Yet the cross and the believer's response are not mystical experiences. When Paul talks of the cross here, he is talking of the significance of the cross as it is explained in the preaching of the gospel. Merely looking at a tattered and broken piece of humanity hanging on a piece of wood, or imagining such with the mind's eye, is of no use whatsoever. It is the cross set within the context of the biblical story of humanity's creation and fall that has significance; and this requires verbal communication. One might add that there is no other way of communicating this message that can bypass the use of words. Neither painting nor mime nor dance is remotely adequate for the message. Only clear, verbal statement of the matter can bring the message home and frame the matter in such a way that the responses can then be either those of faith or of unbelief.

In sum, the Bible not only presents us with a picture of God's relationship to creation and to his people in which words are absolutely crucial means of his presence and his revelation, and are, by obvious implication, completely adequate for such purposes; it also shows us that words are a vital means of communicating the message of God from person to person. Moses preached; Elijah preached; the prophets, major and minor, preached; Christ preached; and Paul preached. All used words to impress the nature and claims of God upon people. Words are clearly the main means of so doing. Thus, any theology that claims to take the Bible as its authority must take the teaching of the Bible on words, and indeed the verbal form of the Bible itself, with utmost seriousness and thus see words as a normative and normal part of Christianity.

Human Nature as a Universal

One of the key points made in chapter 1 is that repudiation of the past is often part of an assumed, and frequently unconscious, repudiation of the notion of human nature as a given. Why should I take the writings of a bunch of dead white men from seventeenth-century Britain seriously, if I am a live, flesh-and-blood African-American woman living in San Francisco at the start of the twenty-first century? What have fourth-century bishops in the eastern Roman Empire to say that is of relevance to the twenty-something owner of a tattoo parlor in today's London? What is there that binds us together—human beings from different times and places—such that there might be some point of useful contact between us? These are good questions; and underlying them is the idea that human nature is a construct of the particular historical, social, and cultural contexts in which we find ourselves.

If the whole notion of human nature is now negotiable within the wider culture such that our mere sharing of a basic genomic structure with other human beings is not an adequate enough foundation upon which to build a larger, more metaphysical notion of human nature, it is important to note that this is not the case in Scripture. The creation account in Genesis makes a series of fundamental distinctions that are important in this regard. First, there is a distinction between Creator and creation. The latter is utterly dependent on the former for its existence and thus is not to be confused or conflated with God. "In the beginning, God" is foundational to all that follows. God is the one constant of existence; everything else is contingent upon his being and action. The world is created and sustained by God; there is no mutual dependency, simply divine priority.

Second, human beings are distinguished from all other creatures. This is evident in a couple of ways: Genesis 1:27 speaks of God creating man "in his own image." Theologians have wrestled over the centuries with what exactly it is that constitutes this image of God, but the details of that discussion need not detain us here. The point to note here is simply this: human beings are distinguished from all other creatures on the basis that they and they alone are made in God's image.

Human beings are also distinguished from all other creatures by receiving a specific mandate from God (Gen. 1:26, 28–30), which effectively places the rest of creation under their control as God's vicegerents. They fulfill a caretaking or overseeing function in creation that is shared with no other kind of creature. Again, what exactly this means is not significant for my argument at this point. It is sufficient to note that the Bible ascribes no similar mandate to any other species.

Closely connected to this is Adam's act of naming. While God himself names Adam, Adam names all other creatures. "And whatever the man called every living creature, that was its name" (Gen. 2:19). Interestingly, we see here that the distinction between humanity and the rest has a certain linguistic aspect to it. Human beings are linguistic beings. We see this further in one other area where humans differ from all other creatures: God speaks to human beings. To be human is to be one who is addressed by God.

We might express this point in slightly different terms: human beings are those confronted by God's revelation, and that confrontation involves a significant linguistic aspect. This is, of course, consistent with what we noted above about the biblical description of God as being a God who, above all else, speaks. It is also surely legitimate to see this linguistic component of human nature as being integral to the notion of the image of God. Of all creatures, human beings are the only ones to whom God speaks and who speak to him in return and also to each other.

The importance of this point is that these aspects of human uniqueness provide a universal context for all human activity. This has various implications. In the discussion of theology, it has become commonplace to talk about two horizons in interpretation: the horizon of the text and the horizon of the interpreter or the interpreting community. This has led in some cases to a radical skepticism concerning the possibility of producing stable and reliable interpretations. We may well share the same text, but if I am a man and you are a woman, or I am white and you are black, is there anything more than our starting point—the text itself—to connect our interpretations? And is it possible to compare your interpretation with mine and decide which of us, if either, has produced a more accurate account of what the text actually says or does?

If we understand human nature as fixed, as something which is not constructed by the individual or by the community but something which is given by God in his address to us, then we are on much more secure ground in moving theological statements from one time, place, or culture to another. Human nature is something which is more basic than gender, class, culture, location, or time. It cannot be reduced to or contained within a specific context such as to isolate it from all else. This is not to deny that context has a huge impact upon who we are and how we think; it is simply to say that all of these particulars that make individuals unique and allow us to differentiate one person from another are relativized by the universal reality of human nature that binds us all together.

Human beings remain essentially the same in terms of their basic nature as those made in God's image and addressed by his word even as we move from place to place and from generation to generation. God remains the same; his image remains the same; his address to us remains the same. The clear inference is that the basic categories that define the relationship between the two (creation in his image, the fall, redemption in Christ, etc.) remain hardy perennials, unaffected at their core by the comparatively trivial accidents of time and space that separate one person from another. Modern culture, for all of its often drab uniformity, prides itself on difference and on kaleidoscopic variety. Whatever the truth of this may be, it does not affect the essential core of identity that binds me together with human beings in modern China and with people in ancient Rome: we are all made in God's image; and he addresses us all through his word.

In short, a biblical understanding of human nature as a universal will temper any talk that seeks to dismiss theological statements from the past on the simplistic grounds that there is nothing in common between us and the people who wrote them. Frankly, it has become rather tedious to read some simpleton who thinks he is a genius dismissing works of theology or literature or philosophy because they were written by "dead [or sometimes living] white males." The status of being dead, white, or male is neither here nor there when it comes to issues of theological truth (and I am inclined to say, of cultural value either). Just because these pundits cannot see beyond race, gender, and whether someone has a pulse does not mean that the rest of us need to cower before their simplistic categories of discourse. Many theologians I read may be dead, white (though hardly the case for Augustine, I should think), and male, but that does not mean they have nothing to say to a live, black female. All humans are partakers of a common human nature. All are addressed by the same revelation of the same God, and all are called to respond to that revelation. Thus, when my student to whom I referred in chapter 1 asked, "What have these Westminster Standards to do with my ministry?" my response ("What has your ministry to do with the church?"), while perhaps a little cutting, was nonetheless rooted in a basic biblical commitment to the idea of universal human nature, a commitment that both the student and I shared.

To return to a passage I have already cited, in 1 Corinthians 1 Paul provides a good example of the relevance and irrelevance of cultural context and conditioning. Here he addresses different reactions to the cross from two very different cultural groups, Jews and Greeks. The Jews, he says, regard the cross as offensive. That is, to use the trendy jargon, their "reader response" to the gospel is that it offends their Jewish sensibilities to think of God as cursed and hanging on a tree. Their cultural context predisposes them to read the cross in this way. For Greeks the case is different. Their reader response is to see the cross as foolishness, as nonsense. For them it is sheer stupidity to claim that God would contract himself to a span and hang and suffer on the cross, and subsequently to claim that this particular act could have universal significance. The Greeks have a different cultural context that gives them a proclivity to read the cross not as offensive but simply as silly or foolish. Thus, the different contexts of the two groups are very important in shaping their responses to Calvary. Nevertheless, the separate reader responses of the Jews and the Greeks, rooted in different cultural contexts, do not subvert the truth of the cross's universal significance and fixed meaning. This is clear from the fact that both Jews and Greeks can be placed into a single category, despite the different responses they have to the cross: they are those who are perishing, simple as that. The correct response for both Jews and Greeks is to see the cross as the power of God to salvation. This is because both groups are at bottom human beings and thus ultimately accountable in the same way to the same God. The things that divide Jew and Greek are of little importance compared to that which binds them together and places them both under the judgment of the cross.

Undergirding this is Paul's own commitment to something else that points clearly to the givenness of human nature and the solidarity of humanity: the function of Adam and of Christ. The logic of Romans 5 and of 1 Corinthians 15 depends upon corporate solidarity. Adam was the representative head of the human race, of a group of individuals who all share something in common, who all have a common nature. Thus with Christ. When he became incarnate, he assumed something which allowed for his identification with others: once again, a common, shared nature. All attempts to deny or to submerge this nature through an overemphasis upon particulars are both unbiblical and ultimately doomed to failure. Human nature is not simply a socio-linguistic construct. It has an ineradicable objective reality; and that reality provides the vital point of contact across cultures, times, ethnicities, genders, sexual orientations, skin colors, and whatever other particular we might care to think up. Indeed, to deny this would be to subvert the theology that Paul expresses in his Adam-Christ parallelism and would thus have dramatic impact upon the nature of salvation. In fact, it would abolish Pauline soteriology in its entirety.

So how does all this apply to creeds and confessions? Creeds and confessions are human attempts to summarize and express the basic elements of the Christian faith. They have been constructed throughout the ages by people from very different contexts but who are all bound together by the shared horizons of God's revelation in Christ and in the biblical text and their own common human nature as readers of that text. This is what gives creeds and confessions a quality that transcends the local conditions of their original composition and that allows us to take them seriously. Of course, it does not guarantee their truthfulness. All creedal formulations are subordinate to Scripture and subject to correction thereby. Like Jews and Greeks, it is quite possible that other human beings' responses to God's revelation can be wrong—utterly wrong. But we should not take seriously childish arguments that, for all of their specious sophistication, really amount to dismissing the relevance of creeds and confessions on the grounds that the authors lived a long time ago, had a different (or the same) skin color to us, or possessed only one X chromosome.

The Church as Institution

Having established the centrality of words to the nature of God and to the revelation of God to humanity, and having argued that there is such a thing as humanity, partaking of a common human nature, to which these words are addressed, there is one more point we need to establish before turning to the biblical evidence for creeds and confessions, and that is the existence of the church as an institution. By "institution" here, I mean a self-consciously organized body of people who identify with a cause (what we now call "church membership") and who acknowledge a structure of ministerial authority.

We noted in chapter 1 that today there is a widespread cultural suspicion of institutional authority. We also noted that this suspicion is somewhat selective, focusing mainly on what we might call traditional institutions, which are rooted in the past and which carry forward ideas and structures from that past. Newer pop culture institutions—talk shows, television, the web, the music industry—wield huge power and enjoy significant, unmerited, and too often uncritical public confidence. Yet the Bible clearly lays out a structure of authority in the church that is traditional in the above sense, in that a key part of its authority lies in the handing on of truth from one generation to the next via established power structures. The biblical church acknowledges authority at a number of levels: the authority of God's revelation, the authority of the past, and the authority and status of those officially charged to transmit the "tradition" from one generation to the next.

In the New Testament description of the church, there is a very close connection between the institutional aspects of the Christian community and the doctrinal ones. Elders and overseers are marked by numerous qualities, one of which is the ability to teach. This is not, of course, the ability to teach in the abstract, as if mere communication skills were the criterion of office-bearing; rather it is the ability to teach a particular content, the gospel of Jesus Christ. Doctrine and structure are thus interconnected in the person of the elder. Indeed, one could approach the subject of the church from either angle, doctrinal or structural. I have simply chosen for convenience to reflect first on the former.

Basic to belonging to the church in Paul's mind are two things to which he refers in Romans 10:9–10:

> If you confess with your mouth that Jesus is Lord and believe in your heart that God raised him from the dead, you will be saved. For with the heart one believes and is justified, and with the mouth one confesses and is saved.

We will return to this passage later when exploring the importance of making a difference between the level of knowledge minimally required for membership and that required for office-bearing.[2] Here I am concerned simply to note that Paul sees credible Christian profession as involving a doctrinal belief (the Christ has been raised from the dead by God) and a public statement ("Jesus is Lord"). Both are laden with doctrinal freight, but Paul does not seem to indicate that massive doctrinal knowledge is necessary for this basic, credible testimony of faith. Nevertheless, it is clear that doctrine—both in terms of belief and content—is still important to this profession, even if in some fairly minimal way. Words and content are thus significant. What Paul does not say is: if you have a warm, incommunicable feeling in your heart and express this by incoherent sounds from your mouth, you will be saved. No. There is propositional content here— publicly expressed in a manner comprehensible to others. Not that this proposition ("Jesus is Lord") in itself saves—one must also *believe in one's heart*—but

---

[2] I am aware that some Christians dislike the whole notion of membership and regard it as unbiblical as it is not mentioned in the Bible. I believe the word "membership" reflects the biblical concept of belonging to the church community. Whether one uses the word "membership" or not is a matter of dogmatic indifference. Clearly Paul presupposes in his letters that there is a Christian community, that people belong to it, and that some people who belong to it act and think in a way that means they should be expelled from the community and not be allowed back until they repent. That seems to me to be all that the modern notion of "membership" is trying to express.

doctrinal confession and personal faith are intimately and inseparably connected with the salvation about which Paul is writing. One's status as a Christian cannot be separated from words.

That membership of the church is connected to doctrine and words is also clear from noting what it is that leads to one's exclusion. In Romans 16:17, Paul writes the following:

> I appeal to you, brothers, to watch out for those who cause divisions and create obstacles contrary to the doctrine that you have been taught; avoid them.

Notice what Paul says here. Contrary to the modern notion that doctrine divides, Paul here says the exact opposite: these people who must be avoided are divisive precisely because they have departed from the true teaching. It is their doctrinal deviance, their departure from true teaching, that makes them sources of division. If Romans 10:9–10 made the positive case for doctrine as a vital part of belonging, here Paul states the other side of the case, that wandering away from sound doctrine means being divisive and ceasing to belong.

Given that belonging to the Christian community has a minimal doctrinal content, it is not surprising that the New Testament also seems to envision that church members will over time grow and deepen in their knowledge and understanding of the Christian faith. Paul, for example, chides the Corinthians that, at a time when he should have been able to treat them as adults in Christ and feed them on solid food, such was their level of immaturity that he could only give them milk as baby food (1 Cor. 3:1). The writer to the Hebrews also speaks of the need to move on from elementary teachings as one grows toward Christian maturity (Heb. 6:1–2). Thus, the bar of doctrinal knowledge is set low for initial belonging; but the expectation is that this knowledge will grow and deepen as the believer matures within the context of the Christian community.

The task of making sure this maturing takes place belongs to the elders/overseers of the church, one of the reasons why there is a difference between qualification for belonging to the church and for holding office in the same. Paul's letters to Timothy and Titus are most important in this regard. Writing at a time when he knows that he is coming to the end of his earthly ministry, Paul's mind is inevitably drawn to what the church leadership will look like as the generation of the apostles, the men specially commissioned by Jesus himself, passes away. Thus, he lays out clear principles by which leaders are to be selected and by which they are to rule the church.

In 1 Timothy, for example, Paul instructs Timothy to stay in Ephesus to make sure that he can combat the false teachers who have infiltrated the church there. It is not immediately obvious what this false teaching is, but it is clearly doctrinal in nature, focusing on myths, genealogies and some form of distorted understanding of the law (1 Tim. 1:3–11). In this context, Paul outlines the qualifications of an overseer (1 Tim. 3:1–7). These include both the ability to teach (which must here mean teach true doctrine, not simply the possession of good pedagogical skills) and also to care for God's church, a qualification which Paul sees as built upon the overseer's ability to manage his own household. The management language he uses is actually picking up on similar terminology in 1 Timothy 1:4 (ESV: *stewardship*) which has clear implications of good management necessarily being connected to true teaching.

The notion of an overseer, then, is connected to the ability to teach true doctrine and to refute those who teach falsehood. In his letter to Titus, Paul presents a similar list of qualifications for elders, which include holding to "the trustworthy word as taught" so that they can "give instruction in sound doctrine" (Titus 1:9).[3] Paul then moves immediately to urging Timothy to "teach what accords with sound doctrine" (Titus 2:1). In short, the doctrinal maturing of the people of God is something that is especially entrusted to particular individuals in the local church who are distinguished, among other things, by their doctrinal knowledge and their ability to teach the same. The seriousness and importance of this teaching function in the church is then underlined by James's comment that not many should aspire to be teachers because teachers will be judged more strictly (James 3:1).

---

[3] I should note here that I regard Paul's use of "overseer" and "elder" as referring to the same office, given the virtual identity of qualifications and functions he lists for each.

Doctrine is so important in the life of the church that it is only to be entrusted to a special category of qualified people.

Given the tendency of the modern West of disparaging age and experience (which we noted in chap. 1), it is worth noting that Paul's vision of eldership is, by modern standards, profoundly countercultural. Not only does competence in doctrine and teaching imply age and experience, the other criteria Paul lays out for joining the eldership surely make this explicit. A young person, for example, will scarcely have a proven track record of managing his own household well or a good reputation with outsiders; and, of course, an elder should not be a recent convert (1 Tim. 3:1–7). All of these criteria imply age and experience, exactly the kinds of things the contemporary world holds in such disdain when it comes to the deeper questions of life. Of course, Timothy himself appears to be relatively young. That is why Paul tells him to let no one despise him because of his youth (1 Tim. 4:12). But Paul would scarcely have felt it necessary to make this comment unless Timothy's age made him a rather stark exception to the typical rule.

Thus, the whole notion of the eldership as described by Paul runs counter to modern tastes: it places a high premium on doctrine, and it typically assumes a mature age and a breadth of experience. Further, to these two countercultural positions, we can add a third: these officers in the church also carry authority and command respect.

Paul states in 1 Timothy 5:17 that the congregation is to have an attitude of respect toward the elders, an attitude which clearly speaks of their authority:

> Let the elders who rule well be considered worthy of double honor, especially those who labor in preaching and teaching.

The attitude of respect that the congregation is to have toward its elders, and the language of "rule" being used to described the elders' function, speak of authority. Elders are not simply appointed as the equivalent of hired hands; they are those who rule in the congregation. If we needed further confirmation of this, we find it in 1 Peter 5, which is reinforced with a Christological reference and a brief statement of congregational responsibilities toward the leaders:

So I exhort the elders among you, as a fellow elder and a witness of the sufferings of Christ, as well as a partaker in the glory that is going to be revealed: shepherd the flock of God that is among you, exercising oversight, not under compulsion, but willingly, as God would have you; not for shameful gain, but eagerly; not domineering over those in your charge, but being examples to the flock. And when the chief Shepherd appears, you will receive the unfading crown of glory. Likewise, you who are younger, be subject to the elders. Clothe yourselves, all of you, with humility toward one another, for "God opposes the proud but gives grace to the humble."

Elder authority is thus ministerial, linked with and subordinate to the rule of Christ. As a result, elders are to be respected by those who are younger because this is one demonstration of the humility and love which is supposed to characterize the church. New Testament teaching on the church is thus opposed to so many of the currents of modern culture: it places a premium on age and experience; it is doctrinal in that it connects to notions of truth and to the teaching of the truth; and it articulates a hierarchical structuring of the church as an institution. Of course, a careful study of all of New Testament teaching on church leadership would reveal that leadership and authority in the church are not to be conceived of in quite the same way as we find in the world around us. Church leadership is to be marked by service to others, by suffering, by a distinct lack of glory and prestige as the world around understands it. It is the church's failure to embody these ideals that has given some traction to those who place organized religion and its institutions under the same cloud of suspicion as secular institutions such as governments and big businesses. But abuse of church office does not mean that church office ceases to be a biblical idea, and it behooves the church to respond to the challenge of her cultural despisers not by capitulation to the culture or repudiation of the Bible's teaching but by repentance, reformation, and a renewed commitment to the biblical notion of church government and authority.

So what has this to do with creeds and confessions? It is to that point which we now finally turn.

A Form of Sound Words

Central to qualification for eldership, we noted, is a good grasp of sound doctrine and the ability to teach it. This is because the church is to be characterized, among other things, by the growth of her people in knowledge. The elders are thus to be *examples* (1 Pet. 5:3), to represent to the people, in doctrine and life, something to which the people should aspire. No wonder they will be judged more strictly, for their lives and words are an important part of the didactic process which leads to congregational maturity.

The teaching aspect is key for another reason, which is profoundly countercultural in the present day: it speaks of the authority of the past. What Paul charges Timothy to do—and remember that Timothy is, in many ways, the archetypal elder of the postapostolic church in New Testament teaching—is to pass on to the next generation the teaching which he himself has received from Paul. Timothy is to be the means of maintaining the apostolic tradition and, by inference, the eldership is thus to be the agency responsible for the passing down of the gospel from generation to generation. This is not to deny the responsibility of every believer to pass on the faith to others, or of parents to teach their children in a manner analogous to the Israelites, with reference to the Passover in Exodus 12; but it is to say that the elders have a peculiar responsibility for this within the church, and that as their authority connects to their teaching, so also their authority connects to the past and to the tradition of teaching which they themselves have received.

This brings us to the next stage of the argument: if words are central to God's identity, to human identity, and to the relationship that exists between the two, then are those words to be connected to a specific content? The answer is simply and obviously, yes. We see this with the example of the Passover, noted above: the children of Israel are not at liberty to explain the ritual actions of the Passover in any way they choose. They cannot, for example, connect the Passover to Noah's flood or Cain's murder of his brother or to some trivial event in their own lives. Instead, they must connect the action very specifically to events that took place with respect to their ancestors in Egypt via an appropriately constructed narrative that offers a correct interpretation of those events from the perspective of God's saving actions. We might also note the same with the cross: while the cross's significance might be understood in a number of acceptable and mutually beneficial ways (punishment of sin, conquest of the forces of darkness, revelation of God's love, etc.), there are also illegitimate ways of understanding the same, such as Jesus dying because he broke God's law or because he failed in his earthly mission. The message of the cross involves a fixed field of meaning that must be respected by those who claim to teach its true significance.

We can easily add to this list. For example, in 1 Timothy 1, Paul attacks those who are using the law as a springboard for speculation about genealogies and for the construction of myths. He dismisses this and stresses to Timothy that the primary function of the law is not as a means for indulging in speculative mythology but as a means for exposing sin and wrongdoing for what they are. Indeed, to expand the list further would be simple but also pointless: if the content of words used in a Christian context is meaningless or utterly negotiable, why did Paul write so strenuously about the truth and about maintaining appropriate standards of practice and belief? All of his letters are driven to some extent by his desire to correct deviant teaching or deviant behavior or some combination of the two.

To summarize what we have argued in this chapter so far: God is a God who reveals himself through actions and words. In his revelation, words have a primary power because they are the means by which he articulates his presence, by which he commands and promises, by which he establishes and defines relationships with his people, and by which he explains the significance of other, nonverbal revelatory actions. To jump forward from Paul to the Reformation, it is why the Reformers made the pulpit central: they saw the verbal proclamation of God as being central to the church, as that which in a sense constituted her very being in the present. That God remains the same, that human beings continue to be made in his image and to face the same fundamental questions in terms of their relationship to him, means that the basic conceptual building blocks of theology and doctrine—that is, descriptions of who God is and what he has done in relation to his people, and what responses he demands from them—remain the same, despite superficial changes of context.

Thus, at the end of his career, as Paul looks to the future of a church without the benefit of the guidance of the original apostles, he instructs his protégé, Timothy, in what elders should be like. At the heart of this description is his emphasis on correct teaching. But what exactly is this teaching to communicate? How does Paul describe it?

In answering this question, it is interesting to note that in the New Testament Paul both speaks of "a form of sound words" when addressing the issue of Timothy's teaching and his continuing fidelity to the Pauline gospel, and also includes in his letters passages that are suggestive of creedal formulation. Important to both of these is 2 Timothy 1.

The ESV translates 2 Timothy 1:13 as "Follow the pattern of the sound words that you have heard from me, in the faith and love that are in Christ Jesus." The King James Version has the more famous rendering, "Hold fast the form of sound words, which thou hast heard of me, in faith and love which is in Christ Jesus." The word for "form" describes a model, form, or standard that is intended to function as a trustworthy or reliable guide. Thus, what Paul is saying here is: Timothy, make sure that your teaching is sound by using the standard of teaching you see in my ministry as the basic rule. The gospel has content, and that content has been ably expressed in the teaching of Paul, teaching of which Timothy has firsthand knowledge.

What is interesting is that Paul does not simply say, "Make sure you stay true to the conceptual content of what you have been taught." Paul also highlights the *form* of the words used here. I suspect there are two related reasons for this: there is both a theological and a pastoral concern. One of the things that teachers in any discipline do is to teach a special vocabulary to their students and instruct them on how to use that vocabulary correctly. This applies to nuclear physicists as it does to investment bankers: each profession has its own special language, and learning the profession is in large part learning the language and how to use it. This facilitates communication between members of the specific profession and allows work to be done properly and efficiently. It also allows for the easy identification of an outsider, or somebody who does not have the requisite competence in the field.

It is the same in the church. The church has developed over time a tried-and-trusted vocabulary to express the concepts she wishes to articulate. The word "Trinity" is a good example of this. The term is found nowhere in the Bible, but it expresses neatly the fact that Father, Son, and Holy Spirit are all equally and eternally God, there is only one God, but that the Father is not the Son, and the Father and Son are not the Holy Spirit. Use of the word thus has a clear theological advantage: it reflects an orthodox concept and it strongly suggests that the user is orthodox. Certainly, if someone starts talking about God as undifferentiated unity or as "Unitarian" or as three separate gods, those familiar with Christian orthodoxy will immediately start to become concerned.

The use of established and accepted terminology also has a second, pastoral purpose: the local elder may not have a theology degree, and the members of the congregation may never have read Athanasius or the Cappadocian Fathers, but when some visiting preacher stands up in their pulpit and starts telling them that the term "Trinity" is a load of old nonsense, or that God is simply one person, end of story, metaphorical alarm bells should start ringing in their heads. They should realize immediately that they are not hearing "a form of sound words," and they will want to find out why the preacher thinks the word is nonsense before inviting him to speak again.

The same applies to a lot of other theological terms and phrases: "incarnation," "atonement," "grace," "total depravity," "election," "justification by faith," "sanctification," etc. Some of these have direct verbal equivalents in Scripture, some refer to concepts that are more disparately expressed. An established, conventional vocabulary for orthodox teaching is thus of great help to the church in her task of educating her members and of establishing helpful and normative signposts of what is and is not orthodox. Not that words cannot have their meaning distorted over time; even Paul faced this issue when he battled over the meaning of grace in Romans or the Law in 1 Timothy. But the fact that there can be abuse of words and slippage of meaning does not mean that the establishment of a normative form of sound words is not a good thing. This is, after all, precisely what Paul was commending to Timothy as he prepared for the end of his own ministry and the continuation of the church under postapostolic leadership. Conspicuously, Paul does not simply say to Timothy, "Memorize the

Old Testament or the Gospels or my Letters" any more than he ever defines preaching as the reading of the same. The form of sound words is something more. Anyone who claims to take the Bible seriously must take the words of Paul to Timothy on this matter seriously. To claim to have no creed but the Bible, then, is problematic: the Bible itself seems to demand that we have forms of sound words, and that is what creeds are.

Significantly, this statement by Paul comes just a few verses after a clear and concise statement of a major part of that gospel content which he wishes Timothy to maintain and propagate:

> [God] who saved us and called us to a holy calling, not because of our works but because of his own purpose and grace, which he gave us in Christ Jesus before the ages began, and which now has been manifested through the appearing of our Savior Christ Jesus, who abolished death and brought life and immortality to light through the gospel. (2 Tim. 1:9–10)

In short, Paul tells Timothy to hold fast to a form of sounds words just moments after providing him with precisely such a form in this basic statement of Christian theology. Here we have God's grace, a basic christology (pre-existent and historical), and an outline of soteriology, all then identified with the good news of the gospel. This is one sentence, but it covers a large amount of theological ground. We might also note in passing that, given the nature of God, of humanity made in his image, and the need for verbal interpretation of the significance of God's saving actions in history, the verbal emphasis of Paul here is hardly surprising. Words, especially words that make a claim to truth, may be very countercultural today, but they are the building blocks of Paul's theology.

This is not the only instance in the New Testament of statements that seem to have a creedal sensibility. Many scholars regard Philippians 2:5–10 as a quotation from an earlier hymn, which Paul borrows to make his point. Regardless of whether that is the case, the unit stands as precisely a form of sound words that serves to offer a clear doctrinal summary of a key aspect of Paul's christology. First Timothy 3:16 also seems to offer a neat summary of Christian teaching. Even more explicit is 1 Timothy 1:15: "This statement is trustworthy and deserving of full acceptance, that Christ Jesus came into the world to save sinners." Here it seems very clear that Paul is using previously established phraseology, a form of sound words, to capture in a nutshell the gospel.[4]

One further aspect of the commission to Timothy to hold fast to the form of sound words is worth noting, particularly in light of the weight given in chapter 1 to the cultural suspicion of history as a source of wisdom. For Paul, by way of contrast, there is an assumption that the correct teaching can be passed on from generation to generation, and that what has happened in the past can be communicated by a form of sound words down through the ages. As he writes to Timothy, this is surely what lies in the background: Paul is at the very end of his apostolic career. Indeed, the time of the apostles is coming to a close, and he needs to set in place structures to maintain true teaching in the postapostolic world. A form of sound words transmitted by eldership is his way of ensuring good management of the household of God. Continuity of teaching is crucial.

This is why elsewhere in his letters he will talk in terms of *tradition*, that which he is *handing on* to those who follow. Thus, in 2 Thessalonians 2:15, Paul says, "So then, brothers, stand firm and hold to the traditions that you were taught by us, either by our spoken word or by our letter." Again the verbal emphasis is clear: these traditions were taught by words spoken or written; and they are to be the norm of life and teaching in the church in Thessalonica. Similar statements can be found in 1 Corinthians 11:2 and 2 Thessalonians 3:6, where Paul makes conformity to the tradition of his teaching a condition for fellowship.

The content of the gospel is thus to be handed on from generation to generation. In today's society, that is in some senses a strange notion. Traditions, say, of computer programming are not passed on. If they were, I would not be typing on my notebook but would be sitting in a room full of machines with spinning spools of tape. There are continuities in technology but they are often less substantial than

---

[4]Other creed-like statements in the New Testament include Romans 1:3–4; 1 Corinthians 8:6; and 1 Peter 3:18–21.

the dramatic discontinuities that scientific and technological break-throughs bring in their wake. Not so with Paul's gospel. This is truly traditional: it has a stable content and it is passed on from generation to generation. Indeed, for Paul, the fact that something was not taught in the past and not passed on as a tradition would presumably have dramatically increased the chances that it was false.

This notion of tradition, of the need to hand on the gospel, is deeply embedded in the nature of the gospel itself. The historical particularity of the history of Israel and of Jesus Christ means that, if the gospel, the meaning and significance of these things, is not passed on from generation to generation, then it remains in a sense trapped in the past. God's saving actions require interpretation and proclamation in order for later generations to have access by faith to them. This tradition is to be regulated by Scripture as the sole authoritative source of knowledge of God's actions; but it is not formally identical with Scripture. It uses forms of sound words, sermons, hymns, and prayers, among other things, in order to pass the message from one generation to another.

Finally, in discussing Paul's teaching on the offices of the church and the true tradition, or teaching, of the same, we should note that failure in doctrine, as in life, brings forth strong words and action from the apostle. In 1 Corinthians 5, Paul instructs the Corinthian congregation to expel the immoral brother and to "hand him over to Satan." What he is describing is deliberate and complete exclusion from the assembly of the saints on the grounds of the man's sexual wickedness. He uses similar language in 1 Timothy 1 regarding the two figures he names as Hymenaeus and Alexander. He has handed them over to Satan, he says, so that they might learn not to blaspheme. He does not tell us precisely what the content of their sin is, but blasphemy is a term used for the trivial abuse of God's holy name, a casually profane attitude to a holy thing. This seems to connect these two figures to the trivialized and false teaching about the law which Paul mentions earlier in the chapter. In short, false teaching leads Paul to dramatic and formal disciplinary action against the ones who are guilty of such.

If Paul himself takes this action in 1 Timothy 1, he urges the local church to take it in 1 Corinthians 5, indicating that perhaps the man there is simply a member of the church, while Hymenaeus and Alexander are office-bearers. Whatever the case, formal action is clearly to be taken when unbiblical morality or doctrine is being promoted by unbiblical life or teaching; and it is in this context that I would read Romans 16:17. This is more than just advice of an informal kind that advises crossing the street when one sees these divisive people while out for a stroll. It is a positive instruction to take steps to make sure that these divisive people are kept out of spheres of influence that would enable them to divide the church. The gospel, as expressed in a form of sound words and handed down from generation to generation, is connected to specific structures of pastoral oversight in the church. This oversight is responsible both for the positive transmission, regulation, and promotion of true teaching and for firm disciplinary action against those whose teaching does not conform to, and thus subverts, the apostolic doctrine.

Conclusion

In chapter 1 I made the point that creeds and confessions are predicated upon the truth of a number of assumptions: the past is important, and has things of positive relevance to teach us; language must be an appropriate vehicle for the stable transmission of truth across time and geographical space; and there must be a body or an institution that can authoritatively compose and enforce creeds and confessions. As I have argued above, the Bible clearly teaches all three elements. In addition, it also seems clear that Paul himself understands that the passing of the Christian faith involves taking history seriously, understanding God as a God who speaks, having (and holding to) forms of sound words, and not simply reading the Bible in the Hebrew or the Greek. Theological synthesis is part of the church's task, and this is facilitated by the development of ways of speaking which are appropriate to the content expressed and the actions being performed.

Thus, there is surely great irony in the claim made by some that they have no creed but the Bible. One can, of course, appreciate the genuine desire which such a claim embodies, to underline the Bible's status as the uniquely authoritative source of divine revelation. We should all be worried about ever allowing a document that is not divinely inspired to carry ultimate authority in the church.

In fact, of course, the legitimate concern underlying the claim to have no creed but the Bible is entirely consonant with the Protestant understanding of Scripture as expressed in those very traditions which place a high premium on the use of creeds and confessions. Indeed, classical orthodox Protestantism coined the phrase *norming norm* to reflect this unique position which Scripture, and Scripture alone, occupies. As the norming norm, the Bible is that by which all other theological statements must be judged as to their truthfulness of content and adequacy of formulation.

The Westminster Confession expresses this point very neatly in chapter 1.10:

> The supreme judge by which all controversies of religion are to be determined, and all decrees of councils, opinions of ancient writers, doctrines of men, and private spirits, are to be examined, and in whose sentence we are to rest, can be no other but the Holy Spirit speaking in the Scripture.

Here we have a confession, which is considered normative in confessional Presbyterian circles, stating very clearly that its own statements and teachings are subordinate to Scripture and to be normed by the same. To use the technical terminology, if Scripture is the norming norm, then creeds and confessions, when adopted by churches as statements of their own faith, are the normed norms.

3

The Early Church

One of the frequent objections to creeds is that the Bible does not contain any. As we have seen, the position is more complicated than that: the Bible does actually contain material which has a creedal tone to it; and the Bible also teaches principles (such as "holding fast to a form of sound words") that can best be honored through the use of something like a creed or confession.

When we move from the period of biblical history into the post-apostolic age, it should come as no surprise that creed-like formulations soon start to appear in Christian literature. Of course, we need to understand that creeds have a twofold aspect: first, there is the content, both conceptual and linguistic, which is designed to serve the transmission of the faith. We might call this the doctrinal concern. Second, there is the normative nature of such creeds as being binding upon the church. This we might call the ecclesiological concern. Historically, it is clear that the two things are closely related but that the former precedes the latter in terms of chronology. The struggle to define orthodoxy is afoot long before the idea that there should be universally binding creeds becomes a significant factor in the life of the church.

The Rule of Faith

The immediate postapostolic period presented the Christian church with a series of obvious challenges. First, the death of the apostles meant a change in leadership and, indeed, in normative leadership structure. The impending challenge of this was presumably one of the driving forces behind Paul's concern in the Pastoral Letters to establish clear criteria for eldership. Conscious that his own time was running short, he wanted to make sure that he was leaving the various congregations of the church in safe hands. Thus, he instructed Timothy and Titus on the kind of men who should hold office and the type of teaching they were to maintain.

This concern for church office continues into the immediate postapostolic period. It is particularly evident in the writings of Ignatius, Bishop of Antioch and in the *Didache*. Ignatius wrote a series of letters to various churches as he made his way to Rome to be martyred, and in these he continually stresses the importance of having an ordained church leader present at any formal gathering of the church. The *Didache*, a text of unknown provenance which may date from as early as the first century, also speaks of leadership in the church and even offers interesting and novel ways of discerning a false teacher. It is arguable that Ignatius's writings are more consistent with later Episcopal or Presbyterian polity while the *Didache* perhaps hints at a more congregational approach; but what is obvious from both is that church government issues are significant topics of discussion in the postapostolic church of the early second century.

The second challenge to the postapostolic church was that of doctrinal content or, to use (for Protestants) a more loaded phrase, the tradition of apostolic teaching, that is, the teaching handed on in trust from the apostles to the next generation. Even within the New Testament, it is clear that there were challenges to such from within the visible company of the church. This again is a factor in Paul's later Pastoral Letters, as he begins 1 Timothy by urging Timothy to remain at Ephesus in order to combat the false teachers and false teaching that has apparently crept in to the congregation. Challenges to the apostolic tradition of teaching only became more severe in the years following the death of the apostles and indeed, arguably continue through to today. We are, after all, living in "the last days," as were those to whom Paul addressed his letters, and such days are marked by conflict with false teachers within the church.

Particularly significant in this regard was Docetism, the idea that Christ only *appeared* to possess real human flesh. The origins of the idea are unclear but probably connect to traditional notions of the inherent inferiority and even evil of matter, and thus of this as something inappropriate to be joined with deity. Various nebulous groups seem to have held this position; scholarship has bracketed them together under the broad category of Gnosticism because of the emphasis on arcane knowledge which often accompanied the denial of Christ's real flesh.[1]

An influential character among the Docetists, though one who lacked the Gnostic emphasis on mystical knowledge, was Marcion, apparently a native of Pontus on the Black Sea who flourished in the middle decades of the second century. His theology was not simply marked by its Docetism, however, but also by its fundamental revision of the notion of the biblical canon. Whilst the formal recognition of the New Testament canon was far from clear or complete in the second century, Marcion was radical even by the standards of his day in the manner in which he rejected the God of the Old Testament as being antithetical to Jesus Christ. Marcion presented the church not only with a challenge to the tradition of apostolic teaching as carried on in the church but he also proposed criteria for textual canonicity that demanded a response. For Marcion, only ten letters of Paul (he appears not to have known or to have implicitly rejected the Pastorals) and a bowdlerization of Luke's Gospel were acceptable as teaching the truth about God's grace.

Thus, if the death of the apostles posed one challenge to the church, the struggle over the tradition of apostolic teaching and the extent and content of the biblical canon were also significant. It is in this context that we find the development of what became known as the Rule (or Canon) of Faith, a summary of the essentials of Christianity that occurs in various verbal forms in the writings of numerous early church fathers. That the Rule appears to have been stable in content

---

[1]A collection of Gnostic texts can be found in English translation in James M. Robinson, ed., *The Nag Hammadi Library* (New York: Harper and Row, 1977).

but different in verbal form indicates that this is not a formal creed with which we are dealing; but the stability of content nonetheless implies that it was attempting to state normative, commonly agreed-upon concepts. It also clearly reflects the doctrinal issues and strains of the time.

We see early adumbrations of the Rule in the letter of Polycarp to the Philippians, chapter 2, and the letters of Ignatius. For example, in chapter 9 of his *Letter to the Trallians*, Ignatius says this:

> Stop your ears, therefore, when any one speaks to you at variance with Jesus Christ, who was descended from David, and was also of Mary; who was truly born, and did eat and drink. He was truly persecuted under Pontius Pilate; He was truly crucified, and [truly] died, in the sight of beings in heaven, and on earth, and under the earth. He was also truly raised from the dead, His Father quickening Him, even as after the same manner His Father will so raise up us who believe in Him by Christ Jesus, apart from whom we do not possess the true life.[2]

It is clear from this that Ignatius is providing a summary of his understanding of Christ, which is shaped by the pressure he feels from certain Docetists who are threatening the church. Hence the repeated emphasis upon the reality of Christ's historical flesh and life. Of course, while Ignatius no doubt regarded what he was saying as universally true, he was not proposing this precise form of words as somehow binding or as representing "best practice" for all churches everywhere. This is similar to the Rule of Faith but, when writers do mention the Rule, the emphasis upon universality and catholicity is more explicit. Thus with Tertullian, the second-century North African theologian, in his *On the Prescription of Heretics*:

> Now, with regard to this rule of faith—that we may from this point acknowledge what it is which we defend—it is, you must know, that which prescribes the belief that there is one only God, and that He is none other than the Creator of the world, who produced all things

---

[2]Ignatius, *Letter to the Trallians*, in *The Ante-Nicene Fathers*, vol. 1, *Translations of the Writings of the Fathers Down to A.D. 325*, eds. A. Roberts, J. Donaldson, and A. C. Coxe (Oak Harbor, WA: Logos Research Systems, 1997), 69. Cf. his *Letter to the Smyrnaeans*, 1.

out of nothing through His own Word, first of all sent forth; that this Word is called His Son, and, under the name of God, was seen "in diverse manners" by the patriarchs, heard at all times in the prophets, at last brought down by the Spirit and Power of the Father into the Virgin Mary, was made flesh in her womb, and, being born of her, went forth as Jesus Christ; thenceforth He preached the new law and the new promise of the kingdom of heaven, worked miracles; having been crucified, He rose again the third day; then having ascended into the heavens, He sat at the right hand of the Father; sent instead of Himself the Power of the Holy Ghost to lead such as believe; will come with glory to take the saints to the enjoyment of everlasting life and of the heavenly promises, and to condemn the wicked to everlasting fire, after the resurrection of both these classes shall have happened, together with the restoration of their flesh. This rule, as it will be proved, was taught by Christ, and raises amongst ourselves no other questions than those which heresies introduce, and which make men heretics.[3]

The basics of the faith are here: creation, Christ, the Holy Spirit, the coming of the kingdom, and judgment. In setting forth these points, Tertullian assumes that he is simply outlining the faith that has been handed down from the apostles.

In similar vein, we find the Rule also articulated in the writings of another second-century theologian, Irenaeus:

The Church, though dispersed through out the whole world, even to the ends of the earth, has received from the apostles and their disciples this faith: [She believes] in one God, the Father Almighty, Maker of heaven, and earth, and the sea, and all things that are in them; and in one Christ Jesus, the Son of God, who became incarnate for our salvation; and in the Holy Spirit, who proclaimed through the prophets the dispensations of God, and the advents, and the birth from a virgin, and the passion, and the resurrection from the dead, and the ascension into heaven in the flesh of the beloved Christ Jesus, our Lord, and His [future] manifestation from heaven in the glory of the Father "to gather all things in one," and to raise up anew all flesh of the whole human

---

[3]Tertullian, *On the Prescription of Heretics* in *The Ante-Nicene Fathers*, vol. 3, *Translations of the Writings of the Fathers Down to A.D. 325*, eds. A. Roberts, J. Donaldson, and A. C. Coxe (Oak Harbor, WA: Logos Research Systems, 1997), 249.

race, in order that to Christ Jesus, our Lord, and God, and Saviour, and King, according to the will of the invisible Father, "every knee should bow, of things in heaven, and things in earth, and things under the earth, and that every tongue should confess" to Him, and that He should execute just judgment towards all; that He may send "spiritual wickednesses," and the angels who transgressed and became apostates, together with the ungodly, and unrighteous, and wicked, and profane among men, into everlasting fire; but may, in the exercise of His grace, confer immortality on the righteous, and holy, and those who have kept His commandments, and have persevered in His love, some from the beginning [of their Christian course], and others from [the date of] their repentance, and may surround them with everlasting glory.[4]

Irenaeus's Rule exhibits the same basic conceptual content as that of Tertullian but, as noted above, it differs in terms of the phrases and forms of expression used. The Rule was thus not a strict "form of sound words" so much as a statement of sound concepts. Further, both men use it as a means of establishing that what they are teaching is the teaching that was passed on from the apostles and has enjoyed universal acceptance within the church as orthodoxy and thus as basis for assessing contemporary teaching. There is therefore a functional similarity to later creeds on this point even if the linguistic and ecclesiastical nature of later creeds is that much more elaborate and fixed. What is undeniable is that Ignatius, Tertullian, and Irenaeus all indicate that the church, from the earliest postapostolic times, continued and developed the Pauline notion of providing clear doctrinal summaries as means of summarizing the faith.

This also points to the major context for the explicit formation of creed-like material in the early church: that of baptism. The very initiation of new Christians into the faith involved both doctrinal content and forms of sound words, not simply a recitation of select Bible verses. These baptismal statements started in their earliest forms as interrogatory documents that required the candidate for baptism to express his or her faith at a personal level. A classic version of this type of creed was the fourth-century Old Roman Creed, the textual

---

[4]Irenaeus in *The Ante-Nicene Fathers*, 1:330–31.

ancestor of the later Apostles' Creed, but baptismal formulae were in use long before that. For example, Hippolytus of Rome (170–236) gives this account of a baptism in his *Apostolic Tradition*:

> When each of them to be baptized has gone down into the water, the one baptizing shall lay hands on each of them, asking, "Do you believe in God the Father Almighty?" And the one being baptized shall answer, "I believe." He shall then baptize each of them once, laying his hand upon each of their heads. Then he shall ask, "Do you believe in Jesus Christ, the Son of God, who was born of the Holy Spirit and the Virgin Mary, who was crucified under Pontius Pilate, and died, and rose on the third day living from the dead, and ascended into heaven, and sat down at the right hand of the Father, the one coming to judge the living and the dead?" When each has answered, "I believe," he shall baptize a second time. Then he shall ask, "Do you believe in the Holy Spirit and the Holy Church and the resurrection of the flesh?" Then each being baptized shall answer, "I believe." And thus let him baptize the third time.[5]

It is clear from this that basic creedal structures were in place, at least locally, for baptismal candidates by 200 AD. The shape is interesting: the structure is basically Trinitarian, the content is the historical matter of the gospels, and the terminus is the eschaton. The skeletal framework of the whole of the Christian story is there.

Baptism also connects to the Rule of Faith. Writing in his treatise *On the Shows*, Tertullian declares in chapter 4 that "when entering the water, we make profession of the Christian faith in the words of its rule; we bear public testimony that we have renounced the devil, his pomp, and his angels."[6] The Rule of Faith thus becomes a brief form of sound words by which the new believer makes public declaration of loyalty to Christ and renounces the world.

One clear and obvious implication of this is that there was some form of Christian education in the background, some form of cat-

---

[5]Hippolytus, *The Treatise on the Apostolic Tradition of St. Hippolytus of Rome*, trans. and ed. Gregory Dix and Henry Chadwick (Ridgefield, CT: Morehouse, 1992), 33–38.
[6]Tertullian, *On the Shows*, 3:81.

echizing or, to use the modern terminology, membership class, which was designed to inform the new convert. Presumably, this education was also shaped by the kind of confession that was given at baptism. Thus, these early creedal formulae had pedagogical importance in the practical, educational ministry of the church.

In sum, the earliest evidence indicates that Christianity deployed forms of sound words to define itself over against challenges to the faith from within the community of those professing in some way to be the true church (e.g., the Docetics) and also over against the non-Christian world (i.e., baptismal confessions). A doctrinal core and a publicly agreed form for the summary of biblical teaching was basic to postapostolic Christianity and clearly consonant with the concerns of Paul as he writes to the church in the Pastorals, worried about church government and life after the apostles have all died.

The Apostles' Creed

Prior to the fourth century, creeds seem to have been primarily local documents. There does not seem to have been any great understanding on the part of the church of the need to produce universally binding statements. From the early fourth century onward, however, there was a growing consciousness of the need for the church to have agreed upon and binding creeds. The most obvious manifestations of this consciousness are the Seven Ecumenical Councils, a number of which will be listed below; but, historically, another creed, the so-called Apostles' Creed, has also enjoyed wide acceptance in the Christian church and continues to this day to form part of the regular liturgical practices of many communions. Though well known, it is worth reminding ourselves of the text:

> I believe in God the Father Almighty, Maker of heaven and earth. And in Jesus Christ his only Son our Lord; who was conceived by the Holy Ghost, born of the Virgin Mary, suffered under Pontius Pilate, was crucified, dead, and buried; he descended into hell; the third day he rose again from the dead; he ascended into heaven, and sitteth on the right hand of God the Father Almighty; from thence he shall come to judge the quick and the dead. I believe in the Holy Ghost; the holy

catholic church; the communion of saints; the forgiveness of sins; the resurrection of the body; and the life everlasting. Amen.

The similarities with the Rule of Faith are obvious, but there is no scholarly consensus on the literary origins of the creed. The first reference to it as the *Apostles'* Creed occurs in a letter from Ambrose of Milan to Rome in 389, a reference that suggests it was clearly of some vintage by that point in time.[7] It probably has its origins in the third century. It was also to continue undergoing development until it was finally formalized by the churches of the West under Charlemagne somewhere around 800 AD.

The Creed is important because it represents a linguistically formalized version of the Rule of Faith. Obviously, it does not contain the key technical language we find in the Nicene Creed, which was designed specifically to protect the full deity of the Son and the Spirit and their equality with the Father; but it does provide the basic bones of the Christian story, from the uniqueness of God through creation and redemption and on to consummation.

So useful has the creed been as a pedagogical tool that it features in many church liturgies. It has also been embodied directly into the catechetical tradition of the church. Medieval catechisms typically used the Apostles' Creed as the framework for teaching doctrine, a tradition that continued into the Protestant tradition at the Reformation. Both Lutheran catechisms and the Heidelberg Catechism for example, include it. Having stated that Christians are saved by faith (Q. 20) and defined faith (Q. 21), Heidelberg Catechism question 22 reads as follows:

> Q: What is then necessary for a Christian to believe?
> A: All things promised us in the gospel, which the articles of our catholic undoubted faith briefly teach us.

The answer to the next question is the text of the Apostles' Creed, which subsequent sections go on to expound in some detail.

---

[7] Ambrose of Milan, Letter 42.5, The Tertullian Project, http://www.tertullian.org/fathers /ambrose_letters_05_letters41_50.htm#Letter42.

In addition to the widespread liturgical and catechetical use of the creed, it has also been the basis for many popular introductions to the Christian faith. Even in the last century, a variety of theologians, from liberal to conservative, have used it as the framework for basic books on Christianity: Wolfhart Pannenberg, Karl Barth, J. I. Packer, and Michael S. Horton are but four of such.

Given the near universal presence of the Apostles' Creed across the Christian spectrum, it is ironic that it also contains one of the most controversial and disputed statements in creedal and confessional history: the clause which states that "Christ descended into hell." This seems to be a statement with minimal biblical foundation and unfortunate soteriological implications, as if Christ's death on the cross was somehow an insufficient act in itself to fulfill the mandate of the Suffering Servant.

In fact, as is so often the case in the history of theology, the creed's offense at this point is based more on a surface reading of the words from a later context than upon their original intent. Thus, a careful exploration of the words reveals that the creed is not claiming anything particularly objectionable at this point. As Reformed pastor Daniel R. Hyde has recently shown, the words simply express the Old Testament prophecies (and thus biblical understanding) of the death and resurrection of Christ.[8] While I will touch on creedal and confessional revision in the appendix, this is an important reminder that we should not abandon a clause in a creed simply because we do not understand it at first reading.

The Seven Ecumenical Councils

While the early church was a most fertile period for church councils and the production of creeds, doctrinal definitions, and dogmatic anathemas, seven councils in particular have historically been accorded singular importance. This is partly because of the foundational nature of a number of them in setting forth basic definitions of God and Christ, and partly because they occurred at a time when the church was arguably institutionally united and thus could make claims to real

---

[8] See Daniel R. Hyde, *In Defense of the Descent: A Response to Contemporary Critics* (Grand Rapids, MI: Reformation Heritage Books, 2010).

catholicity and ecumenicity at least in terms of its membership and legislative scope. These councils are:

> The First Council of Nicaea, 325.
> The First Council of Constantinople, 381.
> The First Council of Ephesus, 431.
> The Council of Chalcedon, 451.
> The Second Council of Constantinople, 553.
> The Third Council of Constantinople, 680–681.
> The Second Council of Nicaea, 787.

The Eastern Orthodox churches refuse to recognize the ecumenical nature of any subsequent council, while the Roman Catholic Church acknowledges fourteen more, the last being the Second Vatican Council (1962–1965). Protestantism, with a different understanding of ecclesiology from either of these communions, has only limited use for a number of the original seven. In fact, it only really engages at a creedal level with the work of the first four councils. These councils produced one major creed, the Nicene, and one important doctrinal formula, the Chalcedonian Definition. Both are important for Protestants, and thus it is very helpful to have some understanding of them in order to appreciate better our own tradition.

The First Council of Nicaea

Emperor Constantine called the First Council of Nicaea (hereafter Nicaea I) to resolve a deepening conflict in the church over the identity of the second person of the Godhead. The church had been wrestling since the death of the apostles with how to articulate the relationship between Father and Son, and these debates came to a head in the fourth century. The crisis is often referred to as the Arian Controversy, after a Libyan presbyter, Arius, whose writings on the subject had brought him into conflict with Alexander, the bishop of Alexandria. Various forces were at play: the need for the Emperor to maintain a unified church in order to keep the empire stable; the struggle for power in the church between presbyters and bishops; and the debate over the nature of the Logos. The latter provided the theological focal point for the political and ecclesiastical struggle.

It is not the purpose of this book to outline in detail the history of individual councils. Our interest here is in the theological and ecclesiastical significance of their contributions. As far as Nicaea I is concerned, its contribution was conceptual/terminological in that it gave the church an important word that shaped the way in which later discussion of the doctrine of God was conducted. This word was "of the same substance" (Gk. *homoousion*) of the Father. The full text of the key clause reads as follows:

> [We believe in] one Lord Jesus Christ, the Son of God, the only-begotten of his Father, of the substance of the Father, God of God, Light of Light, very God of very God, begotten, not made, being of one substance with the Father.

We need to understand a number of points if the significance of Nicaea I is to be fully appreciated. First, the issue of the Son's relationship to the Father may appear to be somewhat abstruse but is actually vital to the Christian faith. How one resolves that issue will decisively affect how one understands creation, salvation, and a host of other theological and practical issues. Is Christ the first act of God's creation? Does salvation involve God condescending to reach down to his creatures or a creature reaching up to God? Can Christ be worshiped in the same way as the Father? Does Christ truly reveal the Father to us? One's response to each of these questions will be determined by how one answers the question about the Logos's relationship to the Father.

In offering an account of this relationship in terms of "substance," Nicaea I ultimately came to set the terms of subsequent debate for this theological discussion and, given the connection between the resolution of the matter at the first Council of Constantinople in 381 (hereafter Constantinople I) and the later discussions of christology proper, also set the terms of debate for understanding the person of the incarnate Lord Jesus. Anyone today who rejects the usefulness of creeds and yet articulates an understanding of God that uses terms such as "substance" is clearly indebted to traditions of theological discussion that are directly rooted in the creedal debates and definitions of the early church. As noted in earlier chapters, we are all subject to the traditions in which we have grown up, both individually and corporately; only those who understand that that is the case, and who have some understanding of how their traditions were formed, can to any degree stand in critical relationship to such traditions.

Second, recent scholarship has demonstrated that the key terminological innovations of Nicaea I did not come to play a significant part in subsequent debate until the 350s. This is related to another point: that the status of Nicaea as an ecumenical creed with normative, binding status on the church was not something which seems to have been intended in any elaborate and self-conscious manner at the time when it met. Nicaea I came to have such significance only in retrospect as the theological and ecclesiastical emphasis came to be placed upon the term *homoousion*.

Indeed, while theologians influenced by the historiography of later fourth-century debates have tended to see the accent in the creed of 325 as on the *homoousion*, recent scholarship has made a very compelling case for regarding this term as a clarification of the statement concerning the Son coming from the Father. The preoccupation with *homoousion* that we find in the later Athanasius and beyond is thus in part a rewriting or at least a new appropriation of the language and intentions of the council.[9]

Further, that the church does not seem to have initially accorded the creed or its language special status and that this started to change in the 350s indicates that it was becoming apparent at this point that normative doctrinal concepts required normative doctrinal language, and that this in turn needed to be connected to the church as an institution to have any meaning. Thus, Nicaea I was to become extremely important because it provoked the church to reflect on the doctrinal content of the gospel, on the need to fashion an extrabiblical vocabulary for expressing this, and on the need for this vocabulary to be established as normative across the church. The fourth century

---

[9]See Lewis Ayres, *Nicaea and Its Legacy: An Approach to Fourth-Century Trinitarian Theology* (Oxford, UK: Oxford University Press, 2004), 110ff.

was giving birth to creedalism, and it was the struggles surrounding the identity of the Logos as expressed in Nicaea I that provided the context and the dynamic for this development.

The Council of Constantinople

The complex struggles—linguistic, theological, ecclesiastical and political—in the half century after Nicaea I culminated in the great Council of Constantinople. While there is debate on whether the creed we commonly now know as the Nicene Creed was actually formulated at the council, tradition ascribes it to such. Certainly it reflects linguistic developments between 325 and 381 in debates over the nature of God, specifically in terms of determining that God can be legitimately described as existing in three *hypostases,* and that the Holy Spirit is fully God. The creed, or at least a slightly modified form of the original, is probably familiar to many Protestants as the Nicene Creed. The title, of course, is something of a misnomer, given that it was only the indirect product of the debates surrounding Nicaea I. More correctly, we should call it the Niceno-Constantinopolitan Creed. The original text reads as follows:

> I believe in one God, Father Almighty, Creator of heaven and earth, and of all things visible and invisible;

> And in one Lord Jesus Christ, the only-begotten Son of God, begotten of the Father before all ages; Light of Light, true God of true God, begotten, not created, of one essence with the Father through Whom all things were made. Who for us men and for our salvation came down from heaven and was incarnate of the Holy Spirit and the Virgin Mary and became man. He was crucified for us under Pontius Pilate, and suffered and was buried; And He rose on the third day, according to the Scriptures. He ascended into heaven and is seated at the right hand of the Father; And He will come again with glory to judge the living and the dead. His kingdom shall have no end.

> And in the Holy Spirit, the Lord, the Creator of life, Who proceeds from the Father, Who together with the Father and the Son is worshiped and glorified, Who spoke through the prophets.

In one, holy, catholic, and apostolic church.

I confess one baptism for the forgiveness of sins.

I look for the resurrection of the dead,
and the life of the age to come.

This creed represents a significant development over the earlier formulations of Nicaea I. First, ecclesiastically this creed enjoyed normative status as definitive of catholic orthodoxy. Indeed, that remains the case to the present day and is the reason why so many churches include it, or reference it, in their doctrinal standards. Of course, the Western addition of the dual procession of the Spirit ("Who proceeds from the Father and Son") at the Third Council of Toledo in 589 has been a source of East/West contention ever since, but, with this one exception, there is no debate about the rest of the creed's teachings.

Second, the creed contains considerable elaboration of the deity of the Spirit and thus represents a more properly Trinitarian description of who God is. This reflects the way in which debates developed in the fourth century. In the 360s it became clear that the issue of Christ's deity was soon going to be definitively resolved, and attention moved to the identity of the Spirit, as we see, for example, in Athanasius's *Letters to Serapion*. It is important to remember that this development was in part driven by doxological/liturgical concerns: why were Father, Son, and Holy Spirit all mentioned in the baptismal formula? In other words, this was no abstract and practically irrelevant discussion. It was connected directly to the most basic liturgical actions of the church.

With attention turning to the Spirit, we find the rise of the so-called Pneumatomachi, those who accepted Christ's deity but opposed ascribing the same to the Spirit. This called forth vigorous polemics on this issue, and the end result was the section on the deity of the Spirit in the creed of 381. Ironically, some did not think that even this statement went far enough: Gregory of Nazianzus, one of the major intellectual forces of the post-Athanasius church world, left the council in a fit of pique, angered that the fathers gathered there had placed insufficient emphasis on the Spirit's deity.

Constantinople is a great example of how the public criteria for orthodoxy can change over time. In the third century, the notion that the Logos was subordinate to the Father was commonplace and not exceptionable; but as theologians wrestled with the implications of this for God, creation, and salvation, it became clear that such was unacceptable as an accurate description of God. A Christ who was less divine than the Father was a Christ who could not save. In order to ensure that the public testimony of the church witnessed to this vital doctrinal insight, the church needed a creedal statement that made precisely this point.

This latter point is very important. One constant question I face in class as a church historian is, "If doctrine develops, does this mean that what unites us to Christ changes over time too?" This is an excellent question and, indeed, a rather obvious one when one is investigating the history of doctrine. Two things need to be borne in mind here.

First, Scripture gives no hint that that which saves changes: it is always trust in Christ that unites one to Christ. Thus, someone who was a believer in the first century is saved in the same way as someone who believes in the twenty-first.

Second, as noted above, the public criteria for what constitutes a credible profession of faith do change over time, as do the standards for office-bearing.[10] As the church reflected upon the identity of Christ and upon Scripture over time, the limitations and inadequacies of certain formulations became more apparent. We noted above that in the third century, the view that Christ was subordinate to the Father in terms of his being was considered acceptable because the implications of that position had not been fully worked out. Once this had been done, and the unacceptable, unbiblical implications of such a position had become clear, the church put in place statements that ruled such views out of bounds. It is not that people who believed in Christ's subordination in the second century could not therefore have been saved—we are all, after all, saved despite some of the things which we believe. It is rather that the church had come to an understanding that to protect and to articulate the gospel, accurate concepts and

---

[10]This distinction between members and office-bearers is extremely important and will be explored in more detail in chapter 6.

appropriate language were necessary, and some of these had to change over time as the inadequacy and abuse of earlier forms became clear.

The First Council of Ephesus

One of the key things to understand about the creedal and confessional development of Christianity is that creeds do not simply offer new doctrinal models and establish new vocabulary with which to solve particular issues; they also generate new problems and questions and set the terms for future debates. We see this in the development from Nicaea I to Constantinople: the debate comes to be shaped by the term *homoousion,* which is not biblical but which is gradually fine-tuned in such a way as to capture the biblical concept of the relationship between the Father and the Son. Once the term is officially adopted, it then plays a constructive part in setting the terms of future debates.

This provides the background to the third ecumenical council, the First Council of Ephesus. Once it has been established that the Logos is of the same substance as the Father and is fully God, the question of how this relates to the humanity of Jesus Christ comes to be proposed in a specific manner: if humanity too has its own substance, how do these two substances, the divine and the human, relate to each other in Christ? And, more specifically, how do the two substances relate to each other in a way that does not create either two persons (albeit occupying one geographical space) or some peculiar blend or fusion of the two substances that leads to the formation of a third substance, which is neither divine nor human? It should be clear that only when the decision has been made to articulate the divinity of the Logos in terms of substance do the problems relating to substance become an issue for church discussion. This is one of the reasons why theology cannot simply be done by reading the Bible: the fine-tuning of concepts and vocabulary is a cumulative and traditionary exercise. This does not mean the results are not biblical, in the sense of being consistent with what the Bible teaches or useful as explanatory devices for understanding the Bible; but it does mean that one will search in vain in the Bible for the terms "Trinity," "substance," or "hypostasis" for example—or, for that matter "conversion experience," "personal relationship with Jesus," "missional," "relational," and "no creed but the Bible!"

Given the resolution of the Trinitarian question provided by Constantinople I, christological questions could now be addressed with the new conceptual vocabulary of substance. It also intensified debates that had surfaced in the years leading up to Constantinople I. Perhaps the most important example of these was the controversy surrounding one of Athanasius's closest allies, a man called Apollinaris, the bishop of Laodicea. Apollinaris had a distinctive view of the person of Christ which was actually condemned at Constantinople I. Put simply, Apollinaris was rightly concerned to defend the full consubstantiality of the Logos with the Father. He did this so radically that he argued that, in the incarnation, the Logos replaced the human soul of Christ. It was a clever resolution to a tricky problem thrown up by Nicene theology: if the Logos is a divine person and unites with human nature, how does one avoid having two persons simply occupying the same space? And if you have two persons in the incarnation, then there really is no incarnation: the divine has not truly united with the human and there can be no salvation.

The problem with Apollinaris's solution, of course, is that on his account Jesus Christ is not really fully human: after all, humans have souls; and if Christ lacks one, then he is not fully human. More acutely, to cite the view of one of Apollinaris's contemporaries, Gregory of Nazianzus, what is not assumed is not healed. If Christ did not assume a human soul, then that vital part of humanity was not saved. Thus, Constantinople I rejected Apollinaris's theology.

If Constantinople I ruled out of bounds the Apollinarian solution, the opposite problem—that of radically separating the divine and human natures in such a way that Christ could hardly be regarded as one person at all—was the next challenge. Again, it is important to see how the question was shaped by previous resolutions: language of substance and hypostasis solved the three-in-one problem but also meant that later discussion would address questions about the incarnation to the biblical text in a manner profoundly shaped by previous creedal agreements and the language they contained.

The First Council of Ephesus addressed this issue relative to the teaching of Nestorius, Bishop of Constantinople. Nestorius objected to the use of the traditional title of "Theotokos" as applied to the

Virgin Mary. Literally, it meant "God bearer." While it is a matter of some debate as to whether Nestorius ever held the heresy that bears his name, his rejection of Theotokos brought him under suspicion of denying the full union of the divine and the human in one person in Christ. Opponents, most notably Cyril, Patriarch of Alexandria, raised concerns about his teaching and after years of controversy, the council at Ephesus condemned Nestorius's teaching and vigorously asserted the unity of the person of Christ.

The importance of the Council of Ephesus is twofold in the history of creeds and confessions. First, it is the last council which the Coptic churches in the East acknowledge as authoritative. Known as monophysite ("one nature") churches, these reject the later teaching of the Council of Chalcedon that Christ has two natures in one person. Second, it effectively closed debate on one issue (the number of persons in Christ), establishing the boundary of orthodoxy on that point, which set the scene and the limits for future creedal discussion on Christ. To be considered orthodox, all subsequent theologians have had to respect that boundary.

The Council of Chalcedon

The last of the early councils which is of major relevance to modern Protestantism is the Council of Chalcedon. The immediate polemical background was the teaching of a man called Eutyches, a monk from Constantinople. Again, there is debate about whether he was a truly innovative heretic or an orthodox figure who simply had great difficulty in expressing himself. Whatever the truth of the matter, he was understood by others to be denying the true humanity of Christ by effectively having it absorbed by the divinity.

The events of the late 440s are politically and ecclesiastically complex, with move and countermove being made by various factions in church and empire. The culminating moment, however, was the Council of Chalcedon, where the following formula was approved as defining the relationship between substances and person in Jesus Christ:

> Therefore, following the holy fathers, we all with one accord teach men to acknowledge one and the same Son, our Lord Jesus Christ, at once

complete in Godhead and complete in manhood, truly God and truly man, consisting also of a reasonable soul and body; of one substance with the Father as regards his Godhead, and at the same time of one substance with us as regards his manhood; like us in all respects, apart from sin; as regards his Godhead, begotten of the Father before the ages, but yet as regards his manhood begotten, for us men and for our salvation, of Mary the Virgin, the Godbearer; one and the same Christ, Son, Lord, Only-begotten, recognized in two natures, without confusion, without change, without division, without separation; the distinction of natures being in no way annulled by the union, but rather the characteristics of each nature being preserved and coming together to form one person and subsistence, not as parted or separated into two persons, but one and the same Son and Only-begotten God the Word, Lord Jesus Christ; even as the prophets from earliest times spoke of him, and our Lord Jesus Christ himself taught us, and the creed of the fathers has handed down to us.[11]

The Chalcedonian Formula effectively puts into place four boundaries for future christological discussion, boundaries which theologians must not transgress in order to remain orthodox: Christ must be fully God; Christ must be fully human: the two natures must not be so mixed together that either disappears into the other or that a third, hybrid nature is produced; and the two natures must not be separated so as to undermine the unity of the one person.

Several points of interest are worth noting here. There is a strong element of negative theology in Chalcedon: it is effectively defining where one must not go with one's christology rather than setting forth a positive definition. That is no bad thing. There is a sense in which the incarnation of the second person of the Trinity in human nature is a deep, unfathomable mystery. One simply cannot give full expression to that mystery in words; but what one can do is map out the theological field in which orthodox discussion can take place by indicating clearly what must *not* be said about Christ if one is to do justice to the biblical teaching about the incarnation. Thus, Chalcedon puts in

---

[11]The Chalcedon Formula, *Documents of the Christian Church*, trans. Henry Bettenson (Oxford, UK: Oxford University Press, 1947), http://www.anglicansonline.org/basics/chalcedon.html.

place boundaries, and any christological formulation that honors those boundaries is thus observing key aspects of biblical teaching necessary for holding to a Christ who can actually save.

Another point is that, as with earlier creedal formulations, Chalcedon generates its own fresh questions which subsequent theologians must address to the biblical text. For example, if Christ is one person and two natures, how many wills does he have? A person typically has one will, one source of motivation, action, etc. Thus, the obvious answer would seem to be that Christ too has one will. This leads to a problem, however: which will does Christ therefore lack—the divine or the human? Or does he have a hybrid will made of the two? If he lacks one or the other, he cannot be said to be fully human or fully divine, depending which will is lacking; if he has a hybrid, he has neither one.

This interesting quandary led the church at the Third Council of Constantinople in 681 to decide that Christ has two wills, divine and human, but that they both work in perfect harmony, with no tension between them at all. Now, at first glance that is a very weird answer to the question. Nowhere in the Bible does it say that Christ has two wills. It is thus tempting to point to this as a bit of needle-headed theological hair-splitting on a matter of no importance and thus a piece of extrabiblical tradition imposed upon the faith.

Yet to draw such a conclusion would be to misunderstand how theology is formulated in and by the church. As noted above, each time one problem is solved, the terms of discussion are changed to take into account the new solution. This solution then generates new questions that the church needs to address to the biblical text and to answer in a manner consistent with that text. Therefore it is only when one understands the history of certain questions that one can understand why the answers given are the appropriate ones.

Thus, if somebody does decide it is nonsense to say that Christ has two wills, one should ask them, "Well, which does he lack?" As soon as the question is asked, the problem should become obvious. One could dismiss the question as ridiculous; but then one needs to go back and effectively rebuild one's christology (and one's Trinitarianism) from the ground up. Given the time, care, and effort of the church in fine-tuning these doctrines in the first place, it is highly unlikely that any other solution will prove less problematic. One can always try, but one then runs the risk of wasting time and ending up with a formula that either does not work as well or for as long or as universally as that which has already been tried and tested across the ages. Indeed, Christian orthodoxy is sometimes the sum of the least number of doctrinal difficulties, complications, and strange statements with which one is prepared to live.

This is an important point to bear in mind, both in terms of creedal formulation in particular and the development of Christian doctrinal formulation in general. Creeds solve one set of problems, but by doing so generate new vocabulary and raise novel questions for the biblical text that then need to be resolved. This is not to say that truth changes over time; but it is to say that the manner and terms in which truth is expressed, along with some of the questions asked, do change. Historical theology, the genealogy of doctrinal discussion and formulation, is thus an important part of Christian education and should be part of every pastor's and elder's background. It should also be a central part of the teaching ministry in all churches.

The Athanasian Creed

The last ancient creed of significance for this discussion is the so-called Athanasian Creed. While this is not an ecumenical creed in the sense of having been produced and ratified by an ecumenical council, it has nonetheless played a significant role in the life of the church, both East and (especially) West. For example, it is part of the liturgy of the Book of Common Prayer and, since the seventeenth century, has featured in Russian Orthodox service books. Thus, it has enjoyed considerable ecclesiastical and liturgical influence over the years.

The name, of course, implies that it was Athanasius, the great fourth-century bishop of Alexandria and champion of Nicene orthodoxy, who was the guiding hand behind its composition. In fact, this is not the case. It was originally of Western provenance, written in Latin by a person or persons unknown. The date is also difficult to establish with any certainty. Its Trinitarian theology clearly indicates that it was composed no earlier than 381; and it is unclear whether the christology it contains places it before, during, or after the Nestorian controversy of the 420s.

The creed articulates standard post-381 Trinitarian orthodoxy and also a careful christology. These are not particularly contentious. What has made it controversial over the years are the two anathemas. These occur in clauses 2 and 44:

> 1. Whosoever will be saved: before all things it is necessary that he hold the Catholic Faith:
> 2. Which faith except every one do keep it whole and undefiled, without doubt he shall perish everlastingly. . . .
> 44. This is the Catholic Faith, which except a man believe faithfully, he can not be saved.[12]

Such anathemas, which were also a feature of the original Nicene Creed, fall foul of contemporary tastes. There is an influential element even within conservative evangelicalism that wants to draw boundaries only by stating the positive, only by emphasizing what is actually believed and thus excluding the heterodox and the heretical only by implication. This is consonant with the spirit of an age where exclusion is seen as a bad thing—and not, as we noted in chapter 1, without good reason in many cases. Exclusion for the sake of elitism or based upon hate and prejudice is deeply wrong and harmful, and the church needs to repudiate such and avoid it at all costs. Yet we cannot as Christians avoid the fact that the faith is always exclusive in some sense, that this exclusivity is expressed in part by public doctrinal commitments, and that the holding of certain positions and the rejection of others determines whether one is included or excluded. As has often been pointed out, of course, one cannot hold to the center of a circle without knowing where the circumference lies. Thus, boundaries, and the drawing of them, are absolutely vital to healthy, orthodox Christianity.[13]

---

[12] Available at Christian Classics Ethereal Library, http://www.ccel.org/creeds/athanasian .creed.html.

[13] This applies both to elaborate confessional statements, such as the Westminster Confession, and to less elaborate examples, such as the doctrinal bases often used for parachurch organizations. The respective bases differ not in the fact of boundary drawing, or the prioritizing of a putative center over boundaries, as if the former is positive while the latter are negative, but simply in the number of boundaries drawn. To adhere to a positive

This is what the author(s) of the Athanasian Creed were attempting to accomplish. In the spirit of other creeds, such as Chalcedon, they used formulations that mark points beyond which the orthodox must not pass; all that they added were specific, explicit anathemas to make sure that readers would fully understand the implications of the matter. Like other ancient creeds, this one was not dealing with trivia or with matters of peripheral relevance to the church. It was dealing with the very identity of God in such a manner that denial of its affirmations placed one's soul in serious jeopardy.

The response, of course, might be that the Athanasian Creed—or that of Chalcedon, or Constantinople, for that matter—seems to demand belief in something that is not explicitly stated in Scripture. But as we saw above, that kind of objection is not a particularly compelling one. What is stated here rests upon the teaching of Scripture, and the implications of that teaching. It is conceptually consistent with the Bible, even if its terminology is actually absent from the same.

Conclusion

Two things are perhaps most striking about the ancient creeds. First is the fact that the early church developed them in the first place. In the century after the death of Paul, we see the rise of the so-called Rule of Faith, which appears to have functioned as a fluid oral summary of the essential elements of biblical teaching, specifically in the face of challenges to orthodoxy. Then, by the middle of the fourth century, given a periodically united Roman Empire and the struggles over the person of Christ, the church as whole came to the conclusion that binding creedal formulas were one way of attempting to establish public criteria for orthodoxy.

Of course, just because a practice is ancient does not mean that it is automatically biblical or appropriate. The visible, earthly church can err, as Protestant confessions themselves make clear; and anyone who has studied the ancient church knows that the seeds of many later practices that evangelicals would reject as unbiblical (for example, the adoration of the Virgin Mary) have their origins during this early

---

statement on any given doctrine is to exclude the opposite, to draw a line which cannot be crossed while claiming to be orthodox.

period of church development. Nevertheless, a case can surely be made for seeing a clear, consistent, and legitimate development from the teaching and practice of Paul in the New Testament through the Rule to the creeds of the fourth century and beyond. Creeds are, after all, simply forms of sound words allied to a church understood not simply as a collection of random believers but as a body with a definite structure and leadership.

The second striking thing is that the early church creeds focus on the most basic building blocks of the faith. The Apostles' Creed is perhaps unparalleled in church history as a succinct statement of the history and significance of Jesus Christ. Its lack of theology proper is only a weakness if one wishes it to do more than that for which it was designed. Thus, one must accept, for example, that it is really no good for keeping out of the church those who deny the Trinity. It is not, after all, an explicitly Trinitarian document, because it does not elaborate the doctrine of God in sufficient detail to do so. But it is still a great account of the basic historical building blocks of the biblical account of salvation.

Moving on to the other ancient creeds from which evangelicals might well profit, we still find the same focus on the very basics of Christianity. What do the Nicene Creed, the Chalcedonian Formula, and the Athanasian Creed have in common? Surely it is this: They all address the most basic of Christian themes—the very identity of God. Whether one agrees with the specific formulations they offer or not, one must agree that the questions they are seeking to answer are perhaps the most basic in Christian theology and, indeed, in the Christian life of the church and of every believer. The meaning of baptism and of Christian praise—praise that ascribes lordship to Jesus Christ—are both wrapped up inextricably in the answer to the question of who he actually is.

This is why these early creeds in particular have enjoyed significant influence throughout the centuries. They do not answer the only questions that are important to the Christian, such as how the individual obtains salvation, but they do address the central point of Christ's identity. Significantly, they also do so in a way that most churches have found to give an adequate account of the Bible's teaching.

With the exception of the Coptic Church's rejection of Chalcedon, Roman Catholics, Eastern Orthodox, and Protestants (Lutheran and Reformed) all accept that these creeds are basically the gold standard for talking about Christ.

The challenge for a "no creed but the Bible" pastor at this point is obvious. If you want to abolish the early church creeds because you regard them as some kind of man-made tradition that stands independent of Scripture or that trumps Scripture's teaching, you are going to need to replace them with something. Further, you are going to need to replace them with something straightaway. The church cannot exist for even the time it takes to say the Nicene Creed without an understanding of who Christ is and, by implication, who God is.

The obvious moves for such a pastor are twofold. He can simply adopt creedal categories without ever actually acknowledging from whence he took them. Thus, he might still use the term "Trinity" and speak of Christ as one person, two natures, with his divine nature being co-equal with the Father. There is a sense in which this is to be welcomed: at least such a pastor is actually teaching his people good, sound theology, even if he is not being exactly transparent or perhaps even self-conscious about where he is obtaining it. To such a pastor, I would simply say that the more one acknowledges the traditions upon which he depends for his theology, the more he is actually able to assess them in the light of Scripture. Ironically, to repudiate creeds but to use their content makes one more, not less, vulnerable to being swept along by tradition, simply because one does not understand that one is actually connected to such.

The second move is the biblicist one of staying as close as possible to the biblical narrative and the biblical categories. Again, there is much that is highly commendable here: what Christians who wish to be biblically faithful do not want their theology normed by the Bible? The problem with this is that, depending on which strand of biblical teaching one chooses to privilege, the results could be disastrous in a number of ways. To emphasize biblical teaching on the unity of God might lead to what is essentially a modalist christology, where Father, Son, and Holy Spirit are the same person of God, just in different time dispensations and modes of being. Or an emphasis on the distinction of Father and Son, coupled with passages that speak of the Father's superiority, might lead to subordinationist christologies, where Christ is somehow less God than his Father. Worse still, the distinction might be emphasized to the point where the result is more than one God.

This is not to say that any of these will be the inevitable result of abandoning or ignoring the ancient creeds. But to avoid them, it is almost certain that the pastor will have to use commentaries or theological books that do connect to the creeds of the early church. It is a simple fact that the church of the first five centuries was the context of a host of doctrinal experiments, whereby different theologians tested different models of God and of Christ to find out which ones did most justice to the Bible's teaching. The Nicene Creed and the Chalcedonian Formula are two key results of that; and the fact they have proved their ability to last for so many centuries as such widely accepted accounts of the biblical teaching is surely not something we should take lightly.

Thus, my response to the biblicist pastor would simply be this: do not precipitately abandon creedal formulations which have been tried and tested over centuries by churches all over the world in favor of your own ideas. On the whole, those who reinvent the wheel invest a lot of time either to come up with something that looks identical to the old design or something that is actually inferior to it. This is not to demand capitulation before church tradition or a rejection of the notion of Scripture alone. Rather, it is to suggest an attitude of humility toward the church's past which simply looks both at the good that the ancient creeds have done and also the fact that they seem to make better sense of the testimony of Scripture than any of the alternatives. The Lord has graciously provided us with a great cloud of witnesses throughout history who can help us to understand the Bible and to apply it to our present day. To ignore such might not be so much a sign of biblical humility as of overbearing hubris and confidence in our own abilities and the uniqueness of our own age.

Of course, as Protestants, we do not believe that the ancient creeds say everything that a church committed to teaching the whole counsel of God needs to say to the world. Those who would see a return to the ancient ecumenical creeds as the answer to later church divisions and as a means of restoring church unity are certainly to be commended for their desire to see Christians united. The problem, of course, is that such a proposal automatically relativizes all later developments. That is great for the Eastern Orthodox churches; it is problematic for committed Roman Catholics and Protestants who may disagree on issues such as justification and the sacraments but yet agree on the fact that these things are important, that Christians need to have convictions on these matters. Thus, for Protestants, discussion of creedalism cannot stop with Chalcedon. It must also address confessional developments in the sixteenth and seventeenth centuries. It is to these we turn in the next chapter.

4

Classical Protestant Confessions

In the period of the Reformation, the church in Western Europe started the process of institutional fragmentation that has continued unabated to this day. If one had been born at the turn of the sixteenth century, one would have considered it inconceivable that the church in the West would not be one and continue to be so. The idea that the church would fragment, let alone that there might even be more than one church in a given geographical area, would not have crossed the mind of any thoughtful person, let alone the many thoughtless people who no doubt existed then as now. Yet one hundred years later, at the turn of the seventeenth century, the Western church was shattered into pieces in the manner with which all Christians today are very familiar.

This fragmentation also involved confessionalization. This term is more than simply a way of referring to the production of theological confessional documents. In the sixteenth century, theology was inextricably bound up with politics: the theological position held by a prince or by a city council had implications for military and political alliances. In other words, theology was very closely tied to territorial politics. Thus, the production of confessions in the sixteenth and seventeenth centuries had dual impulses behind it: theological, because the new churches needed to identify themselves in relation to other emerging communions; and political, as territories and cities needed to define themselves in relation to each other.

Of these two impulses the second is of no real relevance today. Even in a country like England, with an established church presided over by the monarch, theology is of no significance to international relations or to domestic politics, beyond the occasional debate about whether the Church of England should continue to enjoy its special constitutional status, or the predictable complaints from politicians when the Archbishop of Canterbury makes some inept comment about the economy. This does not, however, mean that the other impulse for confessionalization, the defining of one church in relation to another, is no longer relevant, as we shall argue in a later chapter. Nevertheless, it is useful to bear the political aspect in mind as it does help to explain why there was such frenetic production of confessions and catechisms in the sixteenth and seventeenth centuries.

Given the large number of confessions produced during this time, for the sake of space our focus here will be on those which continue to play a major role in the main denominations of Protestantism: the Anglican Articles; the Book of Concord; the Three Forms of Unity; the Westminster Standards; and the Baptist Confession of 1689.[1] Before addressing these, however, it is worth giving a basic narrative of Protestant confessionalization as a whole.

The Anglican Articles

The Reformation in England was shaped by a variety of factors. First, King Henry VIII's break with Rome was not fueled by theology so much as his desire to divorce his first wife, Katherine of Aragon, in order to marry his second, Anne Boleyn. This precipitated a rupture with the papacy, which a number of his counselors leveraged to produce

---

[1]The astute reader will no doubt see that these represent a somewhat narrow slice of Protestantism. There are traditions not represented here: the Anabaptists and the various Arminian groupings come to mind. I have not omitted these groups on the grounds that they do not have a confessional heritage worth examining but simply because my focus is on the central Reformation confessional traditions (Lutheran and Reformed) and the appropriation of this by others (the Baptists); and the basic principles of how and why confessions were produced can be adequately—and concisely—illustrated with reference to these.

a church with a more Protestant face. It was not until the reigns of his son, Edward VI, and then Edward's sister, Elizabeth I (after a brief re-Catholicizing period in between under Mary), that the Church of England was truly secured for the Protestant Reformation.

Second, the ebbing and flowing of Protestant political fortunes on the continent meant that a number of leading Reformation theologians spent time in England and impacted both the liturgy and the theology of Anglicanism. This was particularly true of Martin Bucer, the Reformer of Strasbourg; Peter Martyr Vermigli, the leading Italian Reformer of the day; and John a Lasco, the Polish Reformed theologian. Thus, the Church of England was the product not simply of internal English politics but also of careful theological dialogue with some of the greatest European Reformation minds of the day.

The three towering textual achievements of Anglicanism are the Book of Common Prayer, the Thirty-Nine Articles, and the Homilies. Of these three, the Book of Common Prayer is undoubtedly the greatest liturgical achievement in the English language. In comparison, modern attempts of the same (of which I am aware) seem like wooden verbiage. As with all thoughtful liturgies, it also reflects and embodies a certain theology and was thus crucial in inculcating the same within the congregations who used it. Doctrinally, however, it is the Articles and the Homilies which are crucial to the Church's stated confessional identity.

The Homilies, published in two volumes (1547 and 1571), are a series of thirty-three short sermons that were to be read aloud in church. At the time of the Reformation, there was a key problem relative to personnel: the supply of Protestant ministers could not possibly meet the immediate demand created by the state's allegiance to the Reformation. There is an analogy here with more recent revolutions. When the Eastern Bloc collapsed in 1989–1991, the men and women at the very top of the political power structures were rapidly replaced. It was simply not possible, however, to sweep away in a moment all of the functionaries of the old regimes; this would have created turmoil. Further, it was probably not necessary: the lower down the chain of command one goes, the less likely one is to find ideologically driven people and the more likely one is to find those who simply do their job in order to earn a salary. Thus it was in the Reformation: while church leadership at the top changed when Protestantism arrived, most parishes would have continued to have the same pastors and priests as before. Further, the education of a large Protestant ministry required the prior reformation of educational institutions and the development of faculty and appropriate curricula. Thus, while Reformation at the top might have been swift, Reformation root and branch was a much longer-term project and demanded immediate remedial measures.

Thus, the production of homilies was in part a response to what we might call the pastoral crisis precipitated by the Reformation. The parish priest may well have been an ignorant fellow who could not even name the four Gospel writers, let alone list the Old Testament prophetic books in order, but if he was basically literate then he could feed his people by reading a set homily at each service. The homilies were thus one means by which the Reformation Anglican Church sought to fulfill Paul's mandate of holding fast to a form of sound words and passing on the faith from place to place and generation to generation.

The other theological document was the Thirty-Nine Articles. Originally finalized in 1571, they represent the closest thing the Anglican Church has to a formal confession of faith. The history of the Articles, both in terms of their interpretation and their legal status and application, has been a turbulent one. Most infamously, John Henry Newman attempted in 1841 in Tract 90 of the *Tracts for the Times* to argue that they were susceptible to a reading which could be described as strongly Roman Catholic in tendency. He based his argument primarily on the fact that they had been composed prior to many of the declarations of the Council of Trent and were thus targeted at putative popular misunderstandings of Catholic teaching, not the genuine article. Newman's interpretative gymnastics were ultimately unconvincing even to himself, and he left for Rome in 1845. But the mere existence of Tract 90 is enough to show how problematic is the history of the interpretation of the Articles.

The Church of England's peculiar history also shaped the tone and scope of the Articles. The English Reformation was legislated by a Parliament that was somewhat less than dominated by committed

Protestants. Thus, the exigencies of the political situation meant that there was an evolutionary aspect to the Church's development, given that reformation could progress only at the pace which Parliament would tolerate. As an established Church, it was also important that she should be as comprehensive as possible, even given the need to exclude certain groups such as the Roman Catholics and the more radical Protestant sects. In this way, Reformation Anglicanism did indeed represent a *via media*, a middle way, but not in the sense for which Newman argued prior to moving Romeward. It was not a middle way between Protestantism and Roman Catholicism but rather between Roman Catholicism and Anabaptism. This is otherwise known as Reformation Protestantism. Both of these factors—the need for care and caution in moving the Reformation forward and the need for a comprehensive Protestantism—meant that the Anglican articles were less sharply and elaborately articulated than many other Reformation confessions.

Thus, the articles make clear statements on such hallmark Protestant doctrines as justification by faith, which is addressed in Article 11:

> We are accounted righteous before God, only for the merit of our Lord and Saviour Jesus Christ by Faith, and not for our own works or deservings. Wherefore, that we are justified by Faith only, is a most wholesome Doctrine, and very full of comfort, as more largely is expressed in the Homily of Justification.

Here, the article sets forth in brief the Protestant position on justification and also makes clear that, brief and concise as the statement is, it should be understood in terms of the more thorough explanation of the doctrine in the Homilies. It is also worth noting that this theology informs the liturgy of the Book of Common Prayer. At morning prayer, the minister declares the following:

> Dearly beloved brethren, the Scripture moveth us, in sundry places, to acknowledge and confess our manifold sins and wickedness; and that we should not dissemble nor cloak them before the face of Almighty God our heavenly Father; but confess them with an humble, lowly, penitent, and obedient heart; to the end that we may obtain forgiveness of the

same, by his infinite goodness and mercy. And although we ought, at all times, humbly to acknowledge our sins before God; yet ought we chiefly so to do, when we assemble and meet together to render thanks for the great benefits that we have received at his hands, to set forth his most worthy praise, to hear his most holy Word, and to ask those things which are requisite and necessary, as well for the body as the soul. Wherefore I pray and beseech you, as many as are here present, to accompany me with a pure heart, and humble voice, unto the throne of the heavenly grace, saying after me . . .

This is then followed by the congregational response:

Almighty and most merciful Father; We have erred, and strayed from thy ways like lost sheep. We have followed too much the devices and desires of our own hearts. We have offended against thy holy laws. We have left undone those things which we ought to have done; And we have done those things which we ought not to have done; And there is no health in us. But thou, O Lord, have mercy upon us, miserable offenders. Spare thou them, O God, who confess their faults. Restore thou them that are penitent; According to thy promises declared unto mankind in Christ Jesu our Lord. And grant, O most merciful Father, for his sake; That we may hereafter live a godly, righteous, and sober life, To the glory of thy holy Name. Amen.

Apart from the striking beauty of the prose, what is noteworthy is how Anglican confessional theology is reflected in the liturgy and is thus cultivated and reinforced in the congregation by the same. This is no dry confessionalism, where the theological confession is simply a constitutional document that never touches the people. It is woven into the very fabric of Anglican life.

Finally, it is worth noting article 8, which, in its original form, asserted that the Apostles', Nicene, and Athanasian creeds "ought thoroughly to be received and believed: for they may be proved by most certain warrants of Holy Scripture." Later this was modified to omit the Athanasian Creed, but the basic point remained the same: this Protestant confession was consciously connected to the catholic creedal theology of the early church; it was no innovation but saw itself as in continuity with the great declarations of the patristic church and was thus catholic and orthodox in the best sense of the word. It was striving, if you like, to hold fast to the form of sound words that it had received on these issues.

Of course, the history of the Anglican church is, by and large, a history of failure to apply the Thirty-Nine Articles and to carry forward the theology they contain. The old joke about the Anglican bishop who was perfectly happy to recite the creed as part of the liturgy each week and only had to omit the first three words, "I believe in" in order to do so with integrity has, sadly, too much truth about it to be entirely amusing; but Anglicans have a beautiful confessional-liturgical heritage. If they choose to squander it, that is not the fault of the founders of their church.

The Book of Concord

Of all Reformation Protestant traditions, Lutheranism is, as the name suggests, the one which is most intimately connected with the career and theology of a single individual: Martin Luther. All orthodox Protestants are indebted to him for many things in their own confessions, not least his understanding of justification by grace through faith. But his thought is particularly influential in the church that bears his name.

This influence is reflected in the contents of the Lutheran confessional documents known collectively as the Book of Concord. The Book of Concord was adopted in 1580 by a group of leading Lutheran churchmen, princes, nobles, and town councils as a means of defining their confessional allegiance within the political context of late sixteenth-century Europe. As noted above, the geopolitical aspect of such confessions no longer applies, but the Book of Concord remains the confessional standard for Lutherans around the world. However, as with the other confessions considered in this chapter, the way the Book of Concord is applied varies from denomination to denomination: conservative groups, such as the Wisconsin and Missouri Synods in North America adhere closely to the doctrine the book contains, while the more liberal Evangelical Lutheran Church in America sits more loosely on the same.

The Book of Concord is actually a collection of a number of different writings:

> The Apostles' Creed
> The Nicene Creed
> The Athanasian Creed
> The Augsburg Confession (1530)
> The Apology of the Augsburg Confession (1531)
> The Smalcald Articles (1537)
> Treatise on the Power and Primacy of the Pope (1537)
> The Small Catechism (1529)
> The Large Catechism (1529)
> The Formula of Concord (1577)

Of these documents, three are of patristic origin (the creeds), three were written by Luther (the catechisms and the Smalcald Articles), and three by his colleague, Philip Melanchthon (the Augsburg Confession and Apology and the Treatise on the Power and Primacy of the Pope). They also bear the unmistakable impact of the particulars of the time of composition. The Augsburg Confession was designed to try to win the Holy Roman Emperor, Charles V, if not over to the Protestant cause then at least to a position of tolerance toward it. Thus, it omitted any attack on the pope's authority. As it became clear in the 1530s that Charles could not be won over and that some statement on the papacy was necessary, Melanchthon composed the treatise on the power of the pope. Luther did not subscribe this, not for significant reasons but because a bad attack of a kidney stone prevented his attendance at the discussions. The Smalcald Articles were composed by Luther in order to provide a confessional basis for the Schmalkaldic League, a military alliance of Lutheran princes. The League did not adopt them, but the Articles did ultimately receive confessional status by inclusion in the Book of Concord.

The final document, the Formula of Concord, is the result of struggles for the identity of Lutheranism after Luther's death in 1546. Luther had, of course, been a divisive figure during his own lifetime. In particular, his emphasis on the nonnegotiability of belief that Christ was present according to both his divine and human natures in the Lord's Supper had led to a break with Zwingli and the Reformed at a colloquy at Marburg in 1529. This had subsequently become a key point of dispute between Lutheran and Reformed churches such that the identities of the two communions were determined to a large extent by precisely this issue.

When Luther died in 1546, rival factions quickly emerged among his followers. On the one hand were those who looked to Luther's gentle colleague, Philip Melanchthon, for their lead. These became known as the Philippists, and their hallmark was a greater openness to ecumenism with both Catholic and Reformed, a concessive attitude on whether both natures of Christ were present in the Eucharistic elements, and a more ambivalent attitude to predestination. The other faction, the Gnesio- ("real") Lutherans placed the Real Presence of Christ in the Eucharist at the forefront of their doctrinal concerns and also held a strict line on predestination, consistent with that of Luther in his great work, *The Bondage of the Will* (1525). After years of internecine struggle, the Formula of Concord enshrined Luther's position on the Lord's Supper and therefore represented the triumph of the Gnesio-Lutheran party.

There are many interesting aspects of Lutheran confessionalism. We might note in passing once again the self-conscious way in which Lutherans connect to the early church tradition by including three patristic creeds in their standards. Lutheranism, like other branches of Reformation Protestantism, did not wish to be seen to be innovative, because the faith once for all delivered to the saints did not need innovation. Of course, it is clear from a study of Christianity that there is a sense in which doctrine develops. This is not to say that the gospel has changed; but the way the gospel is articulated has undergone elaboration. The Lutherans understood this but also saw a clear need for connection with the past and thus with the apostolic teaching.

Two further points are particularly pertinent for the argument of this book: the importance of sacramental theology, and the pedagogical impulse behind some of the formulations.

As to the first, sacramental theology, it is likely that nothing so goes against the grain of modern evangelical sensibilities as the confessional attitude to sacraments. Look at any statement of faith by an evangelical parachurch organization and one is very unlikely to find any clear cut statement on baptism or the Lord's Supper. The reason for this is that differences on these are inevitably divisive (at least in the case of baptism) and often regarded as secondary and irrelevant (as is the case with the Lord's Supper and, for the really lax, baptism). This is not necessarily a problem unless, of course, the parachurch group becomes an agenda setter for the church or, even worse, a power-grab organization that functionally supplants the church. Once that starts to take place, the signal is sent that sacraments are not important at all.

Unfortunately, both the Bible and church history witness to the fact that baptism and the Lord's Supper are of vital importance. More ink was spent arguing over the Lord's Supper in the sixteenth century, for example, than over the nature of justification. Further, one cannot really have a church without having a clear understanding of these things. One may, of course, have a clear understanding which is wrong; but it is better to be wrong about them while still knowing they are of importance than not to realize they are important at all.

Minimally, an understanding of baptism is important because baptism is the means of entry into the visible church; and an understanding of the Lord's Supper is important because, minimally, the admission to or banning from participation in the Supper is a basic part of church disciplinary procedure. Thus, churches that have membership and that exert pastoral oversight and exercise discipline must have a position on both baptism and the Lord's Supper. If a church does not have such, then, frankly, it is not really a church. Thus, we may regret the fact that Luther broke Protestantism in two over his contention that belief in the Real Presence was essential to the faith, but it would have been even more regrettable had he agreed to live and let live with the Reformed because he did not see that the matter was at all important.

The second aspect of note in the Lutheran confessional documents is the pedagogical concern. This is most evident in the two catechisms. The very inclusion of catechetical material indicates that pedagogy is dear to the heart of Lutheran confessionalists. As with the Homilies in Anglicanism, so with the Book of Concord: it rests upon a vision for church life whereby the people are slowly but surely educated in the great doctrines of the faith. They are not meant to stay at the level of knowledge they have when they first start to listen to sermons, let alone when they are baptized; rather they are to grow to maturity in the faith, and an important part of that is growth in doctrinal knowledge.

I shall mention this notion again in chapter 6, but here I want to note how this impacts the Lutheran catechisms in one significant way: the use of traditional language. The early sixteenth century was a time of major social change. The rise of cities drew people away from the countryside and thus disrupted traditional ways of life and created new situations of uncertainty. For example, parents faced seeing their children leave home and go far away; those children lost the extended family that had traditionally provided the network for social support. Life was hard and life was uncertain. My guess is that in such times of uncertainty, church was something of a haven of stability: it was just the same as when you were growing up. Thus, for all of the change in the world around, you could always go to church for a bit of the comfort of the routine and the familiar. Then along comes the Reformation. If we believe that such things as vernacular liturgies and sermon-centered worship were greeted with unalloyed delight, I suspect we are naive. Anyone who has ever been in a church where the elders decided to move from a Bible translation hardly anyone could understand to one that everyone finds comprehensible will know that such a process is often met with vigorous opposition. People like things to stay the same; they frequently do not like change, even when that change is really to their advantage.

Thus, in Luther's catechisms, we find the interesting phenomenon of his new theology expressed using the old terminology. Most striking is the retention of the language of "altar" in the context of the Lord's Supper. Lutheran theology is emphatic in stressing that the Lord's Supper is not a sacrifice, not a priestly act directed by men to God, but rather an act in which God condescends to come down to men. Yet the language of altar is retained. The reason is obviously not theological. It would appear rather to be pedagogical, whereby ears used to hearing talk of the altar would not be unduly disturbed by suddenly hearing of the altar referred to simply as a table. Further, in the Augsburg Confession, even the language of "mass" is retained.

Clearly, in this context, there are political considerations: Melanchthon is trying to win over the Catholic emperor. But there is also surely a pedagogical payoff here in retaining familiar language while filling it with new content.

In sum, the Lutheran confessional documents are clearly designed to establish both doctrinal definitions that clarify what the Lutheran church believes and to provide pedagogical material for educating people in that identity. This twofold aspect of confessionalism is evident in the next group of documents to which we turn: the Three Forms of Unity.

The Three Forms of Unity

The Belgic Confession (1561), the Heidelberg Catechism (1563) and the Canons of Dordt (1619) are collectively known as the Three Forms of Unity. They form the confessional standards of Reformed churches that look to the continental Reformation (as opposed to the Anglo-Scottish Reformation) for their origins. The Reformed Church in America, the Christian Reformed Church, and the United Reformed Church are three of the most well-known American denominations that look to these documents as providing their basic doctrinal identity.[2]

The Belgic Confession was the work of a single man, French Protestant Guido de Bres, who was later martyred for his faith. His purpose in writing the confession was to obtain some level of toleration for Reformed believers in the Low Countries (modern-day Belgium and the Netherlands). What started as an attempt to articulate the faith to political powers in the tradition of the Greek apologists came to have much greater significance when it was adopted by the Synod of Dordt (1618–1619) as one of the confessional standards for the continental Reformed churches.

The Heidelberg Catechism was also probably the work of a single man, Zacharias Ursinus, who was a key Reformed theologian in the

---

[2]I am aware that the terms of subscription in each of these denominations are quite different, with the RCA taking a more liberal line, the URCNA being more strictly conservative, and the CRC falling somewhere in the middle. Within the RCA and CRC, however, there are congregations that do adhere more strictly to the standards than their denominations as a whole.

city of Heidelberg. The ruler of Heidelberg in the early 1560s was Frederick III, who converted from Lutheranism to the Reformed faith. That is odd to modern evangelical ears, for the reason noted above: the matter that really divided Lutheran from Reformed, the Lord's Supper, is of little consequence to those who focus simply on a few isolated doctrines which they regard as constituting the gospel and as providing an adequate basis for the Christian life. By contrast, this was a matter with deep theological and political implications in the sixteenth century.

Thus, when Frederick converted, his conversion created various issues in the city of Heidelberg. First, he needed a statement that would allow for the territory to have a confessional identity. Second, he had a divided faculty at his university, where Reformed, Philippists, and Gnesio-Lutherans were engaged in conflict with each other, a conflict which inevitably spilled over into church life and thus into politics. What Frederick determined to do was commission a confession that might form the basis for ecumenical rapprochement between the Reformed and the Philippists, which would isolate and marginalize the hard-line Gnesios.

The result was the Heidelberg Catechism, a document remarkable for its pastoral tone (cultivated with careful use of the first person in the answers) and also for the fact that it pointedly omits any direct teaching on the matter of predestination. Predestination was an issue that divided the Reformed, who maintained varieties of classic anti-Pelagianism, and the Phillipists who, following the later Melanchthon, tended toward a position more concessive toward human free will. Phillipists were also very opposed to preaching on the topic on the grounds that this could create more pastoral problems than it solved.

According to Frederick's introduction, the Heidelberg Catechism was to provide a basis for confessional unity, a model for training youth, and a guide to teachers and pastors to prevent them from adopting doctrinal changes at will. It was thus both a confessional and a peda-gogical document. It was further enhanced as a pedagogical tool when it was divided into fifty-two sections which then became a preaching guide for the afternoon/evening services in Dutch Reformed churches, ensuring thorough doctrinal coverage of the Catechism every year.

The Catechism was adopted by various synods in the sixteenth century and then, like the Belgic Confession, it was formally approved by the Synod of Dordt as an official doctrinal standard of the continental Reformed churches.

The third confessional standard was actually produced at the Synod of Dordt itself: the Canons of Dordt. The Synod was summoned in the Netherlands to address the problems raised by the rising Arminian party. For us, Arminianism is no more than a branch of Protestant Christianity; in the early seventeenth century, Arminianism, as all theological positions at the time, had serious political implications. As a movement that was seen as potentially more concessive to Roman Catholicism at a time when Spain and France were major forces in northern Europe, Arminianism was controversial not simply for its modification of Protestant theology on matters of predestination but also for its implications for domestic and foreign policy.

Again, the politics of Dutch Reformed theology in the seventeenth century are no longer of any relevance today; but the Canons, as adopted by the Synod at the time, remain a confessional standard. These Canons were a direct response to the Five Remonstrant Articles of 1610, set forth by the followers of Jacob Arminius (1560–1609). These asserted a form of conditional election, universal atonement, a modified understanding of depravity, and the resistibility of grace, along with an article that questioned perseverance. Dordt responded by asserting total depravity, unconditional election, particular redemption ("limited atonement"), irresistible grace, and the perseverance of the saints. This became the basis for what is later known as the Five Points of Calvinism, often referred to by the acronym TULIP.

The Canons were thus not intended as anything approaching a comprehensive statement of Christian doctrine and cannot by themselves form an adequate confessional basis for a church. But, combined with the Belgic Confession and the Heidelberg Catechism, they form part of a thoroughgoing exposition of the Reformed understanding of the Christian faith.

As with the Anglican standards and the Book of Concord, the Three Forms exhibit the same concerns for establishing doctrinal identity and promoting doctrinal pedagogy that was so important to Reformation Protestants. In addition, it is also worth noting that Article 9 of the Belgic Confession accepts the teaching of the Apostles', Nicene, and Athanasian creeds. This connection to patristic Christianity is even more explicit in the Heidelberg Catechism, where question 23 asks what articles are necessary for the Christian to believe and the answer is the full text of the Apostles' Creed, which the Catechism then goes on to expound, point by point. The Catechism is thus most intentional in its connection of its Protestant theology to that of the early church. This is holding fast to a form of sound words and preserving and transmitting the tradition in the very best sense of the word.

A couple of other aspects of the Three Forms stand out. Of particularly note is the statement in the Belgic Confession on the church:

> And this holy church is preserved by God against the rage of the whole world, even though for a time it may appear very small in the eyes of men—as though it were completely extinguished.

In America today among many evangelicals, that statement would appear to be nonsense. The church can seem vibrant, robust, and in many cases numerically strong, too. Yet de Bres knew that of which he spoke: he was a hunted heretic who eventually gave his life for the cause. To be reminded that the church is God's creation and lives in the shadow of the cross, and is not to be judged strong or weak by the standards of the world, is both a salutary rebuke to triumphalism and a great encouragement to those who live in parts of the world where the most noticeable aspects of the church are her outward weakness and suffering. Again, this is simply biblical theology summarized in a pithy statement; and having it as part of the confessional statement of the church means that it will be a constant reminder to her people of the realities that attend God's kingdom here on earth.

One other point to make, and something that really marks the Heidelberg Catechism out as a document of great pastoral beauty in the history of creeds and confessions, is the tone and phrasing of the first and last questions:

Question 1. What is thy only comfort in life and death?

Answer: That I with body and soul, both in life and death, am not my own, but belong unto my faithful Savior Jesus Christ; who, with his precious blood, has fully satisfied for all my sins, and delivered me from all the power of the devil; and so preserves me that without the will of my heavenly Father, not a hair can fall from my head; yea, that all things must be subservient to my salvation, and therefore, by his Holy Spirit, he also assures me of eternal life, and makes me sincerely willing and ready, henceforth, to live unto him.

Question 129. What does the word "Amen" signify?

Answer: "Amen" signifies, it shall truly and certainly be: for my prayer is more assuredly heard of God, than I feel in my heart that I desire these things of him.

I never cease to be struck by the beauty of these two answers. Question 1 shows the glorious Reformation Protestant insight into the fact that assurance is to be the normal experience of every Christian believer and not simply the preserve of a few special saints who have been given extraordinary insight into their status before God, as was the medieval Catholic position.

This is a perhaps one of the greatest Protestant insights of the Reformation. We live in an age where conversion to Roman Catholicism is not uncommon among those who have been brought up as evangelicals. There are many reasons for this: some speak of being attracted by the beauty of the liturgy in comparison with what is often seen as a casual and irreverent flippancy in evangelical services; others like the idea of historical continuity, of knowing where the church has been throughout history; still others find the authority structure to be attractive in an age of flux and uncertainty. Whatever the reasons, most Protestants would concede that Rome has certain attractions. Nevertheless, the one thing that every Protestant who converts to Rome loses is assurance of faith.

Recently a student at Westminster Theological Seminary was telling me how he had once found himself on a plane, sitting next to a famous Cardinal. The two of them had a delightful conversation over the course of the flight. Finally the student asked the Cardinal if he was sure of his salvation; the Cardinal shook his head. "Nobody can be certain of that," he declared. The Cardinal (as one would expect) knew his theology. The answer was a good one from the perspective of Roman Catholic theology.

The insight of the Reformation on assurance was key, theologically and pastorally. And, given that it is one thing that every convert to Roman Catholicism from Protestantism must lose, it is worth noting its priority in the Heidelberg Catechism. The answer is so beautifully phrased; and yet if one ceases to be Protestant, one must cease to claim HC 1 as one's own. That is a very high price to pay. Speaking for myself, all of the liturgical beauty of Rome, all of the tradition, all of the clarity of the authority structure (and that clarity is often, I think, more in the eye of the beholder than the Church itself) cannot compensate for the loss of the knowledge that I know I have been purchased by the precious blood of Christ that conversion to Rome requires.

The Catechism's last question, too, is surely beautiful. In it, a wonderful doctrine of God underpins a deceptively simple statement: we can be certain that God is so gracious that he more surely hears our prayers than we actually feel we desire that for which we pray. That is surely a beautiful idea that pulls together numerous strands of biblical teaching and expresses them in a way that captures the reader's imagination. Again, happy is the church that uses a document such as the Heidelberg Catechism to shape its understanding of God and his people. Indeed, anybody who thinks that Protestant confessionalism is a hard, dry creed needs to read the Heidelberg Catechism. Only the willfully stupid or deluded could possibly dismiss such a document along such lines.

The Westminster Standards

The confessional standards of Presbyterian churches around the world were the product of an assembly of church leaders which took place in England from 1643 onward. England was at that time involved in internal warfare, Parliament versus the Crown. This is traditionally called the English Civil War, but it also involved both Scots and Irish and more than one phase of military conflict. Thus, it is now known in some quarters as the Wars of the Three Kingdoms.

The military politics need not concern us here; what was ecclesiastically significant was the fact that Parliament convened an assembly at Westminster to revise Anglicanism in terms of its liturgy and confession. From the very first edition of the Book of Common Prayer in 1549, there had been complaints that it was not Reformed enough; and even its second edition in 1552 retained practices such as kneeling at communion, which were regarded as too reminiscent of Roman Catholicism. In addition, the Thirty-Nine Articles had proved less than adequate for guarding the full-orbed Reformation theology that was dear to the heart of many Protestants. Thus, in 1595, Archbishop Whitgift had drawn up the nine Lambeth Articles as a means of safeguarding the Anglican Church's teaching on predestination. The Lambeth Articles never gained official statement because the process of their composition had upset the monarch, Elizabeth I; but they did continue to have significance. Indeed, in 1615, the Irish Church had formulated its own set of articles, the so-called Irish Articles, both as a means of asserting its own identity and as a means of sharpening its doctrinal commitments. These Irish Articles contained the text of the original Lambeth Articles.

Thus, when English divines were granted Parliamentary permission to revise Anglicanism in 1643, it was against a background of nearly a century of struggle over Anglican identity and mounting evidence of the inadequacy of the original Thirty-Nine Articles to protect the Reformation legacy.

While the Assembly started with a modest brief, the need for Scottish support led, late in 1643, to the signing of a treaty between England and Scotland, the Solemn League and Covenant. This brought the Scottish Presbyterians into the war on the side of Parliament and also a number of Scottish representatives to the Westminster Assembly. From then on, the Assembly became more radical in its program, no longer merely revising Anglicanism but, in terms of confession and practice, rebuilding it from the bottom up. Thus, the Assembly produced, among other documents, not simply a Confession and Shorter and Larger Catechisms but also a Directory for Public Worship, which was intended to supplant the Book of Common Prayer.

The Restoration of the monarchy in 1660 ensured that the Book of Common Prayer was back with a vengeance, and that the Directory for Public Worship became a marginal document even in many Presbyterian circles. But the Confession and the Catechisms remain the basic confessional standards to which confessional Presbyterian ministers and elders, from the United States to Korea and from Scotland to Japan, adhere by solemn vow.

The theology of the Standards is basically consistent with that of the Three Forms of Unity, articulating a theology that is Trinitarian and anti-Pelagian. There are a few differences. For example, Westminster has a much stricter view of the fourth commandment when compared to that of the Heidelberg Catechism. Heidelberg Catechism 103 teaches that the fourth commandment requires the maintenance of Christian education and the prioritizing of gathering for worship on Sunday. In the Larger Catechism, questions 117 and 119, a prescriptive list of things that must and must not be done is provided. The difference here is quite obvious and indicates very different traditions of Christian practice on this point; but, even so, it is arguable that this does not involve any major difference in overall theological substance between the two.

One thing is clear to anyone comparing the Westminster catechisms to the Heidelberg Catechism: the former contain a much greater amount of more thoroughly elaborated theology than the latter. This has helped foster the impression that the Westminster catechisms are less pastoral. There is certainly a sense in which this is true: the consistent use of the first person in the Heidelberg Catechism gives a certain pastoral and personal feel to the whole document. The Westminster catechisms, by contrast, tend to operate more at the level of impersonal propositions. Nevertheless, when one remembers their purpose, the instruction of the faithful in theology, this should not be a matter of great concern. No confessional or catechetical document stands by itself; it is part of an ecclesiastical way of life, one element of our lives as Christians. Thus, the Westminster documents can be taught and used in a lively encouraging way just as the Heidelberg Catechism can be taught in a way that is boring and lifeless.

In addition, the Standards also indicate that the authors were men of acute pastoral insight. For example, the early generations of Protestant Reformers tended to talk as if saving faith and assurance of salvation were so closely connected as to be virtually inseparable. This was undoubtedly in large part a reaction—an appropriate reaction—to the medieval denial that assurance of salvation was at all a possibility for ordinary Christians. Nevertheless, once assurance became a key issue, it was inevitable that it would bring in its wake a whole new set of pastoral problems. As early church theological developments changed the doctrinal map and generated new questions, so did the Reformation. If nobody is expected to have assurance, then nobody will worry about not having it; but tell people they should be assured of their salvation, and you will quickly find that people start to struggle with the issue. Thus, in the chapter entitled "Of the Assurance of Grace and Salvation," Westminster Confession 18.3 says, "This infallible assurance doth not so belong to the essence of faith, but that a true believer may wait long, and conflict with many difficulties, before he be partaker of it." Is this a deviation from the emphasis or teaching of the early Reformers? I am not inclined to think so. Over one hundred years of Protestant pastoral practice has intervened between the inception of the Reformation and the Westminster Assembly. This is not so much a deviation as a modification, based upon the pastoral experience these men have of preaching and teaching Protestantism to their congregations. It is thus also a sign of the pastoral usefulness and sensitivity of the Confession, revealing it as far more than a set of dry propositions that never touch real life and experience.

Further, the Standards do contain much more that is of direct relevance to everyday Christian life. The extended reflections in both catechisms on the Decalogue contain much that is directly practical and thus binds the one who vows to uphold the Standards to particular patterns of behavior. Indeed, one may not like or agree with the teaching on the fourth Commandment in the Larger Catechism, for example, but one could hardly argue that it is not practical or does not have implications for how one lives. Thus, the exposition of both the Decalogue and the Lord's Prayer contain significant applications to the life of the Christian.

In fact, even the Confession itself has some striking practical moments. For example, I have often been impressed by chapter 15.5, which reads:

> Men ought not to content themselves with a general repentance, but it is every man's duty to repent of his particular sins, particularly.

It is fascinating that this is in a church confession. First, it clearly rests upon a specific understanding of God, humanity, and sin. So it is profoundly theological. Second, it makes a clear point about Christian practice, condemning by implication the lazy tendency that we can have as Christians to repent in general terms and let that be sufficient. In other words, it advocates a particular model of the practical outworking of Christianity.

Yet there is still more here: the minister who vows that he believes in, and will uphold, the system of doctrine taught in the Westminster Standards, is thus bound to practice and to teach others to practice this principle. He is, in fact, as bound to this as he is to belief in the incarnation and the virgin birth. In other words, confessionalism is not simply about abstract doctrine; confessions also bind one to certain practices, certain ways of life. This is important to remember when reflecting on the opposition sometimes made between Christianity as a set of beliefs and Christianity as a way of life. For the confessional Christian, it is both: the Westminster Confession, as just one example, makes this very clear. A good confession binds doctrine and life, believing and belonging together, and a minister bound to such a confession by solemn vows must thus honor both sides of that. Good confessions do not undermine but can actually protect the practice of piety.

Before moving to some concluding thoughts, it is worth noting one more confession, the so-called 1689 Baptist Confession. It is "so-called" because it was actually written in 1677, not 1689. However, the Act of Toleration, which opened the way for some freedom of religion for non-Anglicans, was not passed until 1689. Only then could the document become a legitimate part of public ecclesiastical discourse rather than simply the clandestine confession of an underground church.

The Baptist Confession is essentially a slight modification of the Westminster Confession. Inevitably, it articulates a different view of baptism, restricting it to professed believers only, and also affirms an independent polity whereby each particular congregation is fully competent and wholly responsible for its organization and discipline.

I mention the 1689 Confession, not because it makes major contributions to confessional theology but because it is proof positive that Baptists have a confessional heritage. It is not only Roman Catholics, Anglicans, Reformed, and Presbyterians who place high stock in creeds and confessions and who connect these to specific structures of ecclesiastical authority and accountability; it is also some strands of Baptist life as well.

Conclusion

Classic orthodox Protestantism has a rich confessional heritage. Of course, I have only covered a few of the relevant documents, though arguably the selection represents the most influential. As noted at the start of this book, many Protestant churches have their own confessional history; and, while I have restricted myself to those one might characterize as belonging to the mainstream anti-Pelagian Protestant tradition, this is not to deny the importance of Arminian and Anabaptist confessions. My main interest in this book is with the *principle* of confessionalism and not so much with the specific content of particular confessions.

In closing this chapter, however, it is worth making a few observations. First, as noted above, all of the confessional material above stood self-consciously within the basic Trinitarian and christological framework laid out in the early church creedal formulations. There is no indication that the framers of Reformation Protestant confessions were attempting to build theology completely anew. It is clear that the Reformers and their successors were grateful for and appreciative of the theological work of the church throughout the ages. And, while they firmly believed everything—including their own confessional documents—was subject to being normed by the teaching of Scripture, they did not believe that the church's testimony had to be reinvented afresh every Sunday. God had provided them with a church which had a history, and that history was helpful in understanding what Scripture taught.

Second, there is a remarkable degree of consensus among these documents on the basics of salvation. Of course, the objection can be made that I have deliberately selected documents that correspond with each other on key points. Had I included, say, the Remonstrant Articles of the Arminians or the Racovian Catechism of the Socinians, the consensus would not have been nearly so great. That is a fair point, but I would still argue that when one looks at the Book of Concord, the Anglican Articles, the Three Forms, and the Westminster Standards, one is looking at doctrinal standards that cover a vast amount of Protestantism and that have had, and still do have, a large number of adherents. It is thus meaningful to argue for a confessional consensus among these documents on issues such as the nature and being of God, the history of salvation, and the nature of justification. That is quite impressive when you consider that these documents were produced by different people in different cultural, political, social, economic, and linguistic contexts. Indeed, if one were to expand the confessional material to include other documents from the sixteenth and seventeenth centuries, such as the Irish Articles or the Hungarian Confession, the consensus of these basic points would still hold.

Third, there are also significant points of divergence. The most obvious are the differences between Lutheran and Reformed over the presence of Christ in the Lord's Supper. This raises two important points: the importance of honest difference, and the particularity of confessional commitment. And these points in turn highlight the importance of always seeing confessions in an ecclesiastical context.

As to the importance of honest difference, I noted in the first chapter that factors such as fear of excluding somebody often militate against notions of doctrinal precision. The problem, of course, is that the church needs to take a position on certain things. Take baptism, for instance: either it is legitimate to baptize infants or it is not. There is no middle position. Further, one really cannot equivocate on this matter, because the answer one gives has a profound effect on how one understands entry into the church, the Christian life, and the nature of Christian nurture. The same applies to the Lord's Supper: how one understands the Lord's Supper has ramifications for the whole of Christian existence. If the church is the place where Christians receive their nurture and grow together, then there has to be clarity on such issues.

This leads directly to the particularity of confessionalism. Though we might talk about confessionalism as a principle when we refer to churches that hold to clearly stated doctrinal confessions, such churches always exist particularly. In other words, it is not the fact that they adhere to any confession that is the really important thing; it is the fact that they adhere to a *particular* confession. This is an important point because of the recent popularity of the term *confessional* evangelical, a term which I have even used myself.[3] The problem with this terminology is that it is typically used today to refer to evangelicals who adhere to what we might call classical mere orthodoxy: an anti-Pelagian Trinitarianism that also upholds the Reformation teaching on justification. There are two problems with calling this *confessional* evangelicalism.

The first problem is that confessional evangelicalism is not confessional in the classical sense, the sense in which I have used it in this book. That requires commitment to an elaborate confession of the kind that we find in the sixteenth and seventeenth centuries, where a whole lot more than the Trinity, predestination, and justification are defined. In particular, the sacraments were a key element in the development of classical confessionalism, shaped both by the break with Rome and then the split between Lutheran and Reformed. What we have today in confessional evangelical circles is rather an eclectic pick 'n' mix approach to classical confessional Protestantism, where those matters which seem helpful to building a broad evangelical parachurch consensus are highlighted and those matters which divide—and have always divided Protestants—are set to one side as of less importance. Interestingly enough, one would normally assume that those things which have historically divided Protestants for so long are more than likely to be very important precisely because of the history of division they have fostered. It would seem a wholly arbitrary, and in fact counterintuitive move to build a *confessional* consensus by denying or

---

[3] See *The Real Scandal of the Evangelical Mind* (Chicago: Moody, 2010).

ignoring those matters which made confessions necessary in the first place. The use of the term "confessional evangelicalism," *pace* my own previous use of the same, is misleading. Holding to some or all of the Five Points of Calvinism does not make one confessional. There is a whole lot more to being confessional than that, whether we are talking Reformed, Lutheran, Anglican, or Baptist.

Second, the matter of being confessional is inextricably bound up with ecclesiastical commitment. This is clearly implied by the comments above, which make it clear that at the heart of classical Protestant confessions lie ecclesiastical distinctives. Yet it goes further than this: confessions are only really confessions when they are adopted and confessed by a church. This requires at a minimum the existence of office-bearers bound by vow to uphold confessional teaching and structures and processes of accountability to ensure that the confession's teaching is what the church actually proclaims. This is consistent with what we noted in chapter 2 concerning New Testament teaching on the church and her confession of the faith.

Thus, to say that one is a *confessional* Christian requires that one also specify to which confession one adheres and in what specific church context one does so. It is an ecclesiastical term, a churchly concept, which only has real meaning in such a context. To use it outside of a churchly context is to use the term equivocally as it implies a very different relationship to a particular confession than that which exists between a church elder or member and the church's doctrinal constitution. Confessional evangelicalism is simply a conservative form of mere Christianity, not the kind of elaborate ecclesiastical Christianity espoused by Luther, Bullinger, Calvin, or Cranmer.

While all of this can seem rather negative, in actual fact what the Protestant confessions do is simply make explicit what is practically the case in any given church one might choose to attend. Churches are particular; they have particular beliefs and practices; and confessions give expression to that particularity.

5

Confession as Praise

To many modern evangelical ears, the idea of a confession of faith sounds just too cerebral and propositional to have much to do with the idea of Christian praise and doxology. Indeed, given the way in which confessions are most obviously significant in confessional denominations, that is, as judicial documents for deciding who can belong and who cannot, it is easy even for those who delight in them to forget that doxology or praise is a vital aspect of their function. Indeed, we might go further and say that not only is this doxological dimension crucial to their use today; it is also vital to an understanding of how they came to be formulated in the first place. Historically, one could make the argument that Christian theology as a whole is one long, extended reflection upon the meaning and significance of that most basic doxological declaration, "Jesus is Lord!" and thus an attempt to provide a framework for understanding Christian praise. If we fail to make this connection, then our appreciation of the creeds and confessions of the church will be dramatically impoverished as, I would argue, will be our understanding of Christian worship itself.

A moment of reflection indicates why this is the case. The term "Jesus" carries with it a vast amount of implicit doctrinal content. Jesus is not Napoleon or Elvis Presley. The word is not simply a contentless cipher into which the reader can pour any significance she wishes. Jesus's identity is highly particular, involving both his personal biography as a specific individual in first-century Palestine and the wider significance of this biography in the context of the history of redemption as laid out in the events recounted in the Old Testament, along with the interpretation of the same offered therein. Then, the whole notion of lordship is not some given or self-evident term; one cannot simply jump from notions of lordship found in contemporary political societies to an understanding of what it means to predicate this of Christ. Rather, the notion is determined by God's revelation of exactly what the lordship of Christ is. Thus, the basic worship cry "Jesus is Lord!" is in itself a confession in the sense that it is both a public declaration of praise and a public declaration of doctrinal commitment. Arguably, all of Christian theology is simply one long running commentary upon, or fleshing out of, this short, simple, ecstatic cry.

The Bible and Confessional Praise

We have already touched on the significance of Romans 10:9–10:

> If you confess with your mouth that Jesus is Lord and believe in your heart that God raised him from the dead, you will be saved. For with the heart one believes and is justified, and with the mouth one confesses and is saved.

The confessing to which Paul refers here is a public act, and such public acts of confession serve a variety of purposes. There is confessing before the world, the action of witnessing to Christ before the pagan nations. Such is captured by the use of the term *witnessing* to refer to acts of personal evangelism. The Greek word for such witnessing, of course, lies behind the modern word *martyr*. Then there is the public and personal affirmation of truth within the church which marks out the true believer from the impostor. Thus, those who deny with their mouths that Jesus is Lord, or who say Jesus is Lord but deny that God raised him from the dead, are not true members of Christ's church, no matter how likeable or pious they might otherwise be. But there is also the further aspect of confession as praise. For Paul, doctrine and doxology are not separated: the truths of the gospel drive him again and again to praise. And, reading his letters, one is struck time after time by the fact that doctrinal statements are clearly uttered in a manner that expresses the sheer delight and joy Paul has in verbalizing such.

Philippians 2:6–11 provides a good example, where Paul, in pressing on his readers the need for humility, describes the mission of Christ using a form which is arguably that of a poem or hymn, and which culminates in the magnificent declaration that "at the name of Jesus, every knee should bow, in heaven and on earth and under the earth, and every tongue confess that Jesus Christ is Lord, to the glory of God the Father." In ending in such a climactic way, this section of the letter is both descriptive, in that it describes what is the end result of Christ's work, and prescriptive, in that it points the reader toward the praise that such truths should evoke. It is also in itself a superb example of what it enjoins: theological confession as doxology.

To Philippians 2, we might also add 1 Timothy 3:14–16, where Paul is talking about wanting to visit Timothy and then breaks out into a hymn of praise, which also constitutes an outline of some key elements of his christology. In this brief passage, he makes a normative statement about God's revelation, the role of the Spirit in Christ's saving work, the witness of angels, the proclamation of the gospel, the resulting faith, and Christ's ascension to glory in the space of a few brief lines; but this is more than just a set of doctrinal propositions—it is also an act of praise. There is no opposition or difference between doctrine and doxology here: the expression of praise is rooted in, and constituted by, an expression of theology. This is a vital point, and we do well to remember that our creeds and confessions are not simply boundary markers but also that they arise out of a desire to praise God, the content of which praise should be the same as that of said creeds and confessions.

Earlier in the same letter, Paul provides a superb example of how polemic, praise, and doctrinal confession can be intimately related. He is writing to his young protégé, Timothy, encouraging him either to go to Ephesus or to remain there (it is not clear which is the case) in order to refute the false teaching of a group that is having an unfortunate influence within the church. This group has quite probably infiltrated the eldership, since Paul himself excommunicates several of them rather than leaving this to the congregation (1 Tim. 1:20; cf.

1 Cor. 5:5). It is unclear exactly what the content of this false teaching is, but it appears to involve arcane interpretation of the law which has the effect of blunting its basic purpose as that which exposes humanity's sin. Against this, Paul asserts the proper use of the law and then offers himself as an example of God's grace and as a paradigmatic case of the gospel. Then, quite suddenly, he moves from his condition to a statement about the mission of Christ to a doxological outburst:

> The saying is trustworthy and deserving of full acceptance, that Christ Jesus came into the world to save sinners, of whom I am the foremost. But I received mercy for this reason, that in me, as the foremost, Jesus Christ might display his perfect patience as an example to those who were to believe in him for eternal life. To the King of ages, immortal, invisible, the only God, be honor and glory forever and ever. Amen. (1 Tim. 1:15–17)

This passage is a remarkable example of how doctrine, personal testimony, and praise can be wonderfully intertwined in the words spoken by a Christian. There is no opposition here between what Christ has done and what Paul has experienced. More significant from the perspective of this chapter is the connection between theology, polemic, and doxology. In attacking the false teachers, Paul inevitably asserts true teaching as the alternative, but for Paul such assertion can never stand on its own and for its own sake: it moves him inevitably to praise.

Yet there is more: the content of this praise, of this doxological statement, is itself highly polemical. To praise God as King of the ages is to deny the claims of anybody else to ultimate kingship: Paul is thus setting the whole of creation within the context of God's sovereignty. To praise God as immortal is to assert that he and he alone is utterly different from everything else in that only he neither comes into being nor passes out of being. To praise him as invisible is to identify him with the God of the Old Testament who could not be seen face-to-face even by Moses and who must not be represented by an image or an idol. To praise him as the only God is to deny the claims of every other thing to which anybody has or will ever ascribe deity. To give him honor and glory is thus to give him what truly belongs to him and to no other. Paul's polemic leads him to praise; yet his praise is itself ineradicably polemical in its assertions. This, of course, is because praise is rooted in, and expressive of, the identity of God. It is thus always going to be doctrinal and always going to be polemical in a fallen world that flees God and prostrates itself before idols.

All of this reflects the basic conclusion of the argument of the last chapter: that doctrine or dogma is part of the very essence of Christianity. As we noted, statements that posit a gap, or even an opposition, between believing and belonging are fundamentally misleading. Believing is the means of belonging. Thus, to say that belonging precedes believing is to misunderstand exactly what belonging is; and to say that believing is possible without belonging is to attenuate the biblical notion of what exactly it is to believe. In other words, separation of the two concepts in any way produces sentiments which might sound inclusive and aesthetically pleasing but are in fact meaningless gibberish.

In practice, of course, it can be very tempting to make such a separation. In the Reformed constituency, the accent upon correct and precise doctrine can lead to an intellectualism that separates doctrine from doxology in a manner that is unfortunate and unbiblical. In other branches of the Christian church, an overemphasis on experience or activism or particular aesthetic forms can lead to the relegation of doctrine to a secondary position or even worse. This side of heaven it is unlikely that any church or congregation will ever achieve the perfect balance; but being aware of the problems and pitfalls does help us to be more self-critical and more aware of the potential weaknesses and temptations to which our particular traditions might be peculiarly vulnerable.

Thus, if true Christian believing and true Christian belonging are two sides of the same coin, inextricably joined together, then praise that expresses the content of belief is the means by which such belonging is given public expression; and this brings us back to creeds and confessions as being normative guides to Christian doctrine and also, in this context, to the content of Christian worship.

Early Creeds and Christian Praise

The worship aspect of creeds and confessions is evident in the early church. The *Didache*, a document possibly dating from as early as the late first century, gives an account of what should be said in a worship service. Baptism is to be performed in the name of the Father, Son, and Holy Spirit (*Didache* 7). That is scarcely surprising, given that it is clearly part of the biblical mandate relating to baptism. When it comes to the Lord's Supper, however, a more elaborate liturgical formula is used that carries with it significant doctrinal statements which are more elaborate than the simple biblical words of institution (*Didache* 9). Most significant in this regard is the prayer of thanksgiving after the meal:

> We give you thanks, Holy Father, for your holy name which you have caused to dwell in our hearts, and for the knowledge and faith and immortality which you have made known to us through Jesus your servant; to you be the glory forever. You, almighty Master, created all things for your name's sake, and gave food and drink to men to enjoy, that they might give you thanks; but to us you have graciously given spiritual food and drink, and eternal life through your servant. Above all, we give you thanks because you are mighty; to you be the glory forever. Remember your church, Lord, to deliver it from all evil and to make it perfect in your love; and gather it, the one that has been sanctified, from the four winds into your kingdom, which you have prepared for it; for yours is the power and glory forever. May grace come, and may this world pass away. Hosanna to the God of David. If anyone is holy, let him come; if anyone is not, let him repent. Maranatha! Amen.

This liturgical statement is shot through with solid doctrine: God as Creator and sustainer; God as Savior; God as protector; God as the object of praise; God as the one who will gather his church; God as eternally powerful and glorious. There is also an underlying note of historical continuity in the reference to David. This is magnificent theology which bears comparison in content with both the summaries of Christianity in the Bible itself and the Rule of Faith, and weaves all of this into the liturgical action of the church in her praise and worship. Doctrinal statement and doxology are correlative developments within the church and we must not lose sight of the latter in our reflections upon the former.

The development of Trinitarian and christological discussion was driven in part by the need to give a coherent account of the worship cry "Jesus is Lord!" as well as the use of the names Father, Son, and Holy Spirit in that most basic of Christian worship actions, baptism. These points should not be dismissed lightly. Indeed, it is surely most helpful when reflecting on the development of Trinitarian discussions to keep in mind that the matrix out of which such developed was that of the public worship and witness of the church. There is surely no more basic action in worship than the declaration of Christ's lordship; and the Christian life, in all of its practical and doctrinal richness, starts with the simple act of baptism. Indeed, to return to the language of believing and belonging, baptism is the practical avenue to "belonging" for all Christians everywhere. Thus, the Trinitarian controversies of the early centuries are nothing if not heated debates about the nature of Christian worship and the nature of Christian belonging. They may well embody at times rarified linguistic distinctions and apparently dry discussion of very fine points of difference, but this should not blind us today to the very practical and doxological orientation of the underlying currents of the debates.

In light of this background, anyone tempted to criticize the Nicene Creed, or even the Athanasian Creed, for being too abstract, propositional, or polemical, should take note of the comments of John Henry Newman in his *Lectures on Justification*:

> I grant that the Athanasian Creed certainly may be taken by careless readers to imply that orthodoxy is the ultimate end of religion; but surely it will seem otherwise on due consideration. For no one can deny, looking at it as a whole, that it is occupied in *glorifying* Father, Son, and Holy Ghost, in declaring their infinite perfections; so much so that it has sometimes been considered what it really is in form, a Psalm or Hymn of Praise to the Blessed Trinity, rather than a Creed, as the Te Deum is. Nay, this is its characteristic, not only in its general structure, but in its direct enunciation of the Sacred Mysteries; which is put forth not as an end in itself, but evidently in order to glorify

God in His incomprehensible majesty, and to warn us of the danger of thinking of Him without reverence.[1]

Newman wrote this in the context of his own internal struggles with Anglicanism and his conflict with the religion of his youth. Thus, he probably had in mind the nineteenth-century evangelicals when he wrote this passage, given their deep suspicion of church creeds and their prioritizing of feelings and emotions at the expense of doctrine for the Christian life. Such a separation of doctrine and Christian experience was, arguably, a species of liberalism, in which human religious psychology is definitive of Christianity. We tend not to see evangelicalism in terms of liberalism because of its public adherence to supernaturalism and our tendency to associate liberalism with varying degrees of antisupernaturalism. Yet we must remember that liberalism is not primarily a rejection of the supernatural; it is a reconfiguration of the nature of Christianity in such a way as to highlight religious psychology or experience and downplay or marginalize doctrine. For Newman, unlike the evangelicals in his polemical crosshairs, the identity of God as God is absolutely fundamental, and the praise (and experience) of God by his people arises out of, and is completely dependent upon, that identity.

We might update Newman here by saying that we should not allow our understanding of creeds to be narrowed and even distorted by a modern cultural aesthetic which prioritizes sentiment over dogma, and which finds distasteful such propositions, claims to absolute truth, and the corollary of rejection of error. Such things were not always regarded as antithetical to doxology and praise as is now the case, a point made with typical clarity by Newman in the above passage. The identity of whom we praise actually informs the content of how we praise him.

It is perhaps worth noting at this point that, with all of the current debates about the nature and meaning of biblical inerrancy, we must not allow a legitimate desire to maintain the propositional truth content of the Bible to obscure the fact that the Bible cannot be reduced to a collection of truthful propositions. It contains, among other things, promises, commands, praise, lament, and histories, all of which are

---

[1] John Henry Newman, *Lectures on Justification* (London: J. G. and F. Rivington, 1838), 362.

not important simply for their referentiality but also for the aesthetic forms in which they are expressed. One danger of a vigorous defense of inerrancy is that it can lead (ironically) to an unbiblical prioritizing of one aspect of the Bible over all else. Nevertheless, all of these literary genres and actions rest upon who God is and what he has done and promised to do. The identity of God is foundational to, and constitutive of, the content and forms of biblical revelation and that is foundational to, and formative of, the Christian response in praise and worship.

This point cannot be stressed enough with regard to doxology: the identity of God has priority over the content of Christian praise. We see this in the Psalms, where who God is and what he has done permeate their language. There are churches (most notably the Reformed Presbyterian Church) that restrict their public praise to the singing of nothing but canonical Psalms precisely because they take very seriously the need for correct forms and content of congregational address to God; the use of hymns of human composition always runs the risk of introducing ideas into the mix that are not biblical at all.[2] True praise of God arises out of an accurate understanding of who he is and involves correct statement of what he has done and does do, in terms of doctrinal content and form of speech. We know that it is legitimate to ascribe glory to God because Scripture teaches that God is the one to whom glory is to be ascribed and offers a picture of the believer's life in which such acts of ascription are a normal part of existence. That is the biblical paradigm that we see in the Psalms and in the many doxological outbursts of Paul and others. A faulty understanding of God and how to respond to him can only lead to praise that is to some extent inadequate in both motivation and expression.

An analogy with human relationships seems apposite: if I approach my wife, all four feet nine-and-a-half inches of her, and treat her as six feet tall, asking her to get the rice from the top shelf in the cupboard, then it is arguable that, however good my intentions in such a request

---

[2] I should note here that I am not personally an exclusive psalmodist, though I have strong pastoral and aesthetic sympathies for the position. I also share the concern that nothing should be said in praise which is inappropriate and that the most obvious way to do this is to sing good translations of the Psalms.

might be, there is some level of dysfunction or delusion in our relationship. I can only relate to my wife correctly as I understand who she is. Likewise, she was born in the 1960s and trained as an elementary school teacher; thus, if I thank and praise her for successfully winning the Second World War all by herself, my comments may be flattering in the extreme, but they are absurd, ridiculous, and out of touch with reality. Such would not be true praise at all: it would be a false action, whether I was aware of its falsity or not. There is a necessary connection between truth and praise.

This is where creeds can play such a vital role in a church's praise, a point that many communions have recognized throughout their history in their very acts of public worship. Thus, both the Apostles' and the Nicene creeds have often found a place within the historic liturgies of the church, as things either to be said or to be sung by the congregation as part of its gathered worship. Some might criticize this action for stressing doctrine at the expense of some nebulous concept of "worship," but that would be to misunderstand the nature of the connection between doctrinal statement and doxology. In reciting the creeds, the purpose is not simply to declare a set of propositional truths. Rather, the action is somewhat richer than that: to state the obvious, in reciting the words of the creeds together, each member of the congregation publicly identifies with every other member in expressing a corporate unity of belief in a common gospel. They are also expressing their common belief with every other Christian throughout history who has used these words to witness to Christ. Further, they are reminding themselves and each other of who God is and what he has done. In other words, the creeds, in liturgical context, become a means of fulfilling the public declaration that Romans 10 demands of believers: the confession (a document) becomes a confession (an act of pointing toward Christ before the church and the world).

The Creeds and Trinitarian Worship

In this context it is worth particularly noting one thing which the ancient creeds do and which is often a weakness in contemporary church life: they highlight the fact that God is Trinity. One might ask why this is important. Is the Trinity not a somewhat complicated and arcane idea, the fruit of the metaphysical wranglings of churchmen in the early centuries and not something that connects to modern life? As noted above, this is not the case: the Trinitarian discussions find their origins in the realm of the church's doxology, and the creeds are in part the product of this. Further, the Christian life is Trinitarian by its very nature. As God the Son is the One sent by the Father and empowered by the Holy Spirit to carry out his work as Mediator, thus salvation is deeply rooted in the Trinity and has what one might call a definite Trinitarian shape. The facts of the gospel are necessarily Trinitarian facts.

Further, the identity of the Christian as the one united to Christ gives each individual Christian a Trinitarian identity: united to Christ by the Spirit, we enjoy communion with God as our Father. The answer to "Who are you?" when asked of a believer must thus elicit a Trinitarian response. Further, what applies to the individual believer applies even more strongly to the church as a body. Paul uses various terms for the church: the body of Christ, the temple of the Holy Spirit, the household of God. Each of these carries with it obvious Trinitarian weight, for neither Christ, the Spirit, nor God can be adequately conceived of without being understood as Trinitarian, first, last, and always.

In addition, we should remember that the very initiation rite of the Christian church, baptism, is itself Trinitarian in form. As Christ's ministry starts with the Father acknowledging the Son and anointing him with the Holy Spirit, so the Great Commission specifically requires baptism in the name of the Father, Son, and Holy Spirit. The Christian's identity is nothing if it is not Trinitarian.

Given this, the Trinity should be a doctrine that both shapes our worship and pervades our worship. Sadly, in many churches this is not the case. There may be an official statement somewhere which indicates that the congregation is committed to Trinitarian doctrine, but all too often there is little sign of this commitment in what actually happens during a worship service. Indeed, having attended the funeral of a Unitarian friend a few years ago, I was struck at how much of what passes for Trinitarian Christian worship would have seemed entirely consonant with the Unitarian service which I witnessed that day.

There is no silver bullet that fixes this problem. The pastor and elders of each church need to be very intentional in how they integrate the identity of the Trinitarian God into the worship service. Trinitarian doctrine can be hard for people to grasp. The Trinity is revealed in Scripture, but it is also something that cannot be comprehended by finite creatures. It is apprehended and believed but it is not fully understood. Thus the teaching of the doctrine needs careful thought and preparation. Elders need to choose hymns and songs that reflect good biblical, Trinitarian theology; they need to make sure that the public prayer is explicitly Trinitarian in its content; they need to work hard at ensuring that the overall liturgical shape of the service does justice to each member of the Godhead; and the minister in particular needs to make sure that his preaching involves careful and clear articulation of God as Trinity.

Most of us will tend, if we are not careful, to emphasize either the unity of God or the threeness of God and thus present an imbalanced view of his being; we thus need to be very self-conscious in our Trinitarianism. This is where, I would suggest, the input of good elders becomes crucial. Listening to the minister each week, the elders should be well-qualified to note imbalances in the theology expressed in the public worship of God.

One other obvious way we can press this issue home, of course, is to use the creeds in our liturgy. By reciting the Nicene Creed together on a Sunday, we remind each other of the identity of God in Trinitarian terms. It is a form of sound words, and the corporate recitation of the same reinforces it in our minds. Of course, such recitation is not in itself enough: it needs to be connected to clear teaching. If the standard level of what is done in a worship service is set at that which the newest, least informed Christian can understand, we are doomed to remain forever in spiritual infancy. As Christians, we should expect worship always to be a learning experience. That requires us not only to call ministers who are able to stretch us theologically; it also means we should fill the worship service with material that draws us on to maturity. The creed is one such thing: it takes a few minutes to memorize and recite but a lifetime to master. Thus the rest of the worship service must connect to, expound, and reinforce its teaching. Some churches will no doubt do this better than others; but even the most theologically impoverished church that uses the creed in its worship can rest assured of one thing—its worship is distinctively different, distinctively *Christian*, when compared to anything that happens in a Unitarian service.

Creeds, Liturgy, and Formalism

If recitation of the creed does not itself guarantee that the congregation will understand what they are saying, some might object to this practice on grounds that are often lodged at liturgy in more general terms: the use of liturgy leads to a mere formalism and outward show that is simply going through the motions of praise without ever actually engaging the hearts and the minds of the congregants.

Of course, the most obvious riposte to this objection is that the Bible itself contains liturgies or set prayers. The Psalms and the Lord's Prayer are only the 151 most obvious examples of such; there are others if you find that number to be too few to build a persuasive case for liturgy upon. Yet even if, for the sake of argument, we were to bowdlerize the Bible or pretend that these things did not exist, we could still make a compelling case for set forms in worship.

In a sense, criticism that claims that forms lead to formalism is vulnerable to the same kind of arguments I have already made against the "No creed but the Bible!" brigade. All Christian churches have liturgies in the same way that all Christian churches have creeds. Tell me the kind of church you attend and I can probably make a good guess about what shape the service will take and what kind of language will typically be used, however "spontaneous" the church may like to think it is. The only real point of difference between churches on this issue is the level of self-consciousness and explicit formality with which they are held. Few, if any, churches have completely anarchic services. A High Anglican from Oxford, UK, attending a snake-handling church in Alabama may think that what she sees is anarchy, but the likelihood is that this Sunday's service actually looks very much like last week's. The lack of explicitly stated forms does not mean that the same basic routine is not followed, week in, week out.

I have sometimes heard people from other churches criticize the structure of the service in my local church for not being "spontaneous" enough. Now, spontaneity is an interesting category. First, it is not immediately obvious to me where one would go in the New Testament to find it as a hallmark of genuine Christian worship. Nowhere does Paul tell people they need to be more spontaneous, or commend them for being so; on the contrary, his strictures in 1 Corinthians seem to arise out of a concern that the church there is not, to use his phrase, doing things decently and in order. The danger with spontaneity, one would imagine, is that it could very soon become just a byword for chaos and anarchy.

Second, it often appears that people use the term not to mean spontaneous in the sense of off-the-cuff, ad hoc, or improvised, but rather to refer to nontraditional liturgical structures and hymnody. Thus, a service with contemporary praise-band music, where nobody but the worship leader is entirely sure how many times the chorus or song is to be repeated, is deemed to be "spontaneous." Yet, when one reflects upon this scenario for a moment, this is surely not really all that "spontaneous" after all. It is preplanned by somebody and, unless everybody is singing different words to different notes (not an entirely unprecedented event in the history of local churches, I am sure), it is also using set forms of some kind. Call them hymns, choruses, songs, tunes, or melodies: their form and content is fixed in advance of the spontaneity of the service.

A pastor friend once told me of a charismatic church in his neighborhood that had invited him to attend a service. The worship leader afterward asked him if he had noticed how spontaneous the worship was compared to the comparatively staid worship at my friend's Welsh Baptist Chapel. My friend asked the charismatic leader when he typically decided on what songs to sing on a Sunday. By the previous Thursday at the latest, was the response, so as to allow the music team time to practice. My friend responded that he never told his organist what hymns he was going to use until the Saturday afternoon, and that he was thus "forty-eight hours more spontaneous" than the charismatics. It is a simple fact: if you use a song book or pre-prepared overheads or PowerPoint to guide the worship at your church, the level of true "spontaneity" is obviously somewhat limited. Add to the mix some-body actually leading worship—whether formally or informally—and again, spontaneity is more of an appearance than a substantial reality.

Thus, as just noted, the New Testament does not actually seem to put any premium on spontaneity as an essential component of authenticity, and so I would suggest that we should not worry too much about either. It is more likely that it is significant for us because of our culturally-conditioned understanding of what makes us and our actions "authentic" (itself as slippery a concept as "spontaneity"). Modern society puts great stock in the idea that what makes us who we are is our individual self-creation and self-determination. That lies at the heart of consumerism, for example. Yet, whether right or wrong socially, it is certainly irrelevant biblically when it comes to worship. Individual self-creation and self-determination are not only irrelevant to Christianity and its various practices, they are arguably antithetical to it as well. It is not what distinguishes me from my fellow human beings which is really significant; it is what unites me to them. I am made in the image of God; I am fallen and sinful and in need of a redeemer; and my salvation is found only in and through the work of the Lord Jesus Christ. Those are truths that apply to me as to every-body else. And my response in worship, whatever particular culture I belong to, must reflect those commonly shared realities. That is why a common confession in a creed is a good thing: it makes the point that my faith is the faith of the other people in the church—both today and throughout the ages.

Of course, one must immediately concede that the recitation of a creed can become a mere outward formality. There is no point in denying such an obvious point. Yet creeds are not unique in this: in much the same way, the singing of a familiar hymn or praise song can easily be a mere outward, mechanical act as well. Even our extemporary prayers can be formalities. Think of how you pray in public, and reflect upon how similar many, if not all, of those prayers are, as you draw upon the same kind of vocabulary and idioms to give expression to your thoughts and longings. How much real spontaneity is there even in our spontaneous prayers? The difference between the contemporary praise songs we sing and the prayers we pray and the creeds we recite is this: hymns are usually the product of a single person; our prayers are the products of our own religious self-consciousness; but the great creeds of the church are corporate products which have been tried and tested by the church across the world and down through the centuries. They carry the authority of the ages behind them. Of course, that does not mean they stand above or even on a par with the Bible in terms of their authority, but it does mean that they are still most significant church documents. Further, the long pedigree that the ancient creeds in particular have as liturgical documents, to be used by the corporate church in her acts of public praise, should also encourage us to think very carefully about how we might tap into such a rich stream of Christian practice.

Thus, let us make sure that when we criticize the recitation of creeds for its formalism we lay the blame where it truly belongs. If such recitation is mere formalism, it is not the fault of the creeds themselves. They are no more to blame for being used in a merely formal manner than Shakespeare can be blamed if people use copies of his plays to blow their noses. Nor is this formalism the fault of the church that establishes such use of the creeds in its worship services. Every church has its liturgy; that in itself does not determine whether the liturgy will be used well or badly. Any set form of words—from a hymn book to a prayer book to a creed—is vulnerable to formalism. Thus, if the creed is read in a merely formal manner, it is the fault of the congregation or of the individual who does so, in the same way that it would be if a hymn or psalm or chorus were sung in the same manner. The use of an established form of sound words is no more vulnerable to formalism than the use of speciously spontaneous alternatives. Creeds are merely a tool for achieving a desired end; it is up to the elders of the church to make sure that their use does not degenerate into mere empty recitation.

The Threefold Aspect of Creedal Doxology

In the Anglican Book of Common Prayer communion service, the corporate recitation of the Nicene Creed takes place right after the minister has read from the Epistles and the Gospels and immediately before the sermon or the homily. The Word of God has been read;

the Word of God is about to be preached; and here, in the moment that bridges the two points, the congregation express their corporate faith in who God is and what he has done. It is a very important part of the service, as it involves the whole of the body of Christ in a positive, active capacity.

We might characterize this corporate action as having a threefold significance. It has a significance at the congregational level whereby all the members remind each other of the identity of God. It has a significance at the level of the congregation's relationship to the broader culture in that, like Paul's doxology in 1 Timothy 1, the church as a gathered body is explicitly, publicly, and defiantly denying the claims of all other pretenders to the divine throne. And it has a significance in terms of God in that it represents the ascribing to him of that glory and honor which is his alone. Further, we might conclude by saying that this one action—reciting the creed—is actually all three of these at one and the same time and that the distinctions we draw between them are entirely formal, since each one inevitably implies or involves both of the others. It is a stunning act of countercultural rebellion on behalf of God. Each of these three points is therefore worth exploring.

Creeds Offer a Corporate Summary of the Bible's Teaching

One of the great complaints of ministers and elders today is the comparative theological and biblical illiteracy of congregants compared to previous generations. We live at a time where levels of basic literacy (the simple ability to read) and accessibility of reading matter (whether printed or "virtual") are at historically high levels. Yet we all know that people seem to read less and are certainly less familiar not only with the Bible story as a whole but even with individual stories within Scripture. Part of the reason for this, at least in the West, is that biblical stories no longer pervade the wider culture as they once did. One pressing pastoral concern, therefore, is how churches should address such lack.

The issue of basic biblical literacy in terms of familiarity with particular Bible stories obviously needs to be addressed from the pulpit, in Sunday school classes, in small group meetings during the week, and through the cultivation of habits of family and private devotions.

Two short Bible readings and one thirty-minute sermon each Sunday will not solve the problem.

The other issue—how to give congregants a grasp of the overall message of the Bible and the gospel—must also be addressed using these same means; but the risk is that each of these approaches can still fail to give an overarching framework. The current habit of expository preaching, where a book is preached passage by passage, is perhaps something of an improvement on the older habit of preaching verse by verse, in that it does allow for more of the Bible to be covered in the space of a year's worth of sermons; but, even so, it can end up offering a rather narrow slice of the Bible's teaching and leave people vulnerable to developing a fragmented or fundamentally unbalanced theology. There is an obvious need for a helpful framework as a basic part of theological education at the very outset of the task and at every step along the way.

The recitation of a classic creed can be of immense help here. A creed—whether the Apostles' or the Nicene—provides in succinct form a clear statement of the identity of God and of Jesus Christ and a summary of the key points of Christ's work. God is Creator; God is Trinity; Christ is incarnate God; he lived, died, rose again, and is ascended into heaven; he will come again in judgment; there is a divine creation called the church; there is an initiation rite called baptism; there is forgiveness of sins; there is eternal life. As the congregation recites this each week, they are surely learning, or being reminded of, the cardinal doctrines of the Christian faith, and that is a vital part of church life. As Paul notes in 1 Timothy 1, it is these simple truths that are the foundation of a pure heart, a good conscience, and a sincere faith; and these in turn are the foundation of that which is the purpose of good teaching: love and the good stewardship of the things of God.

Of course, these creeds are not exhaustive summaries—what "summary" ever can be such?—but they do offer neat, concise frameworks within which the preacher's detailed expositions can be placed. The person who knows the creed knows the basic plotline of the Bible and thus has a potentially profound grasp of theology. In a world where the exigencies of employment have made a high level of transience and fluidity in congregations into something which is the norm rather the exception, it becomes ever more imperative that ministers and elders think very self-consciously about how they can ensure the proper education of the congregants.

There is also a useful connection to more elaborate, confessional material here. Catechisms in particular can be used in the worship service to ensure a congregation is exposed to the sweep of Christian doctrine. This can take two forms. As noted in chapter 4, the tradition of the Dutch churches from the sixteenth century onward was to devote the second service on a Sunday to a sermon based on questions in the Heidelberg Catechism, and to work through the whole document systematically in the course of a year. While this did lead to laziness and tedious repetition in some instances, the principle of covering the key catechetical doctrines in a fairly short space of time is surely a good one. In the present time, with highly mobile congregations and the lack of general theological and biblical literacy upon which to build, the idea of allowing a catechism to guide topical preaching has much to commend it: as a fixed scheme, it prevents the preacher from merely dealing with those areas about which he is peculiarly passionate, and it allows him and his fellow elders to know which doctrines have been specifically addressed from the pulpit and when. Of course, some congregations may not like the idea of preaching on the catechism rather than the Bible, but because that is really a false dichotomy, there should be no real tension here. Frankly, if people object to the idea of catechetical preaching, the minister should simply do it by choosing biblical passages of relevance to the doctrine of the day and not create problems for himself by telling his congregants that he is preaching on the catechism. Pointing them at each sermon's end to a relevant section of a catechism might gently introduce the church to the idea of the catechism's usefulness. Such an act could well reap dividends in terms of the thoroughness of doctrinal coverage that is thereby facilitated.

The other way in which catechisms can be useful in a worship service is to use them as part of the liturgical action. I have been at a number of church services where a question from a catechism was read by the minister and the response of the congregation was the relevant answer. This has a number of points to commend it. First, it familiarizes the congregation with the chosen catechism and fulfills the idea of instilling a form of sound words into the minds of the people of God. Second, when done thoughtfully it can be an obvious element in the drama of the service: a catechetical passage on the law is appropriate before a prayer of confession; a passage on the gospel as part of the words of assurance; a passage on the doctrine of God or Christ or salvation as a basic confession of faith and offering of praise to God, etc. Catechisms are only dead and dry documents if one chooses to make them so. Given that a good catechism bursts with beautiful statements about who God is and what he has done, with a little thought and care they can enrich the dramatic action that should characterize the Christian worship service.

Creeds Are Countercultural

The recitation of a creed in a worship service is one of the most countercultural things that Christians can do. It is an act of defiance, if not even of actual revolution. First of all, of course, we must be persuaded that worship is meant to be countercultural: the seeker-sensitive services of the eighties and nineties, the more recent passion for offering traditional, contemporary, and even jazz worship as options in ostensibly the same church, and the tattooed chic and candles of emergent eclecticism are all ultimately predicated on the notion that worship services are not meant to be countercultural so much as contexts where the idioms of the wider culture are co-opted and Christianized. Sometimes this assimilation to the wider culture is arguably only at the level of aesthetics, but the underlying emphasis in each case is not on countercultural protest but, on some level, of rapprochement between church and wider context. In fact, this type of approach has no real foundation in Scripture. It is obvious that worship services must have some connection to the wider culture (language, location, etc.), but no biblical writer expends any real energy reflecting on contextualization. It would seem that such matters have produced a veritable industry in the modern church world but were very low on the list of the New Testament writer's priorities, possibly because they regarded them as of minimal importance and matters of mere common sense.

Instead, the one description of an unbeliever's reaction to a Christian worship service occurs in 1 Corinthians 14:23–25. Here a properly ordered service has the result of causing the unbeliever to be convicted and to fall on his face to worship God and to declare that God is indeed truly present there. There is no evidence here of any attempt to make the unbeliever comfortable, and the reaction would seem to indicate that, in fact, the exact opposite is the case: the church is simply being the church. Its one concession is that it is worshiping in a public language accessible to the unbeliever, and the rest, as they say, is history. It is clearly not the similarity of the church to the world that is the key to this drama; it is the difference that the unbeliever finds so striking.

Thus, worship is not defined by its proximity or assimilation to the wider context. Instead, worship from its earliest manifestation in New Testament times has been marked by protest against the wider culture. That is why Christians have often been persecuted throughout history. You do not find yourself being persecuted unless you are a threat to others; and you are not a threat to others if you are basically in agreement with them or if you contextualize yourself in such a way as to be indistinguishable from the world around you. Christians in first-century Rome and twenty-first-century China were/are persecuted because they represented something threatening, strange, incomprehensible, and unassimilable to the dominant powers of the day.

This aspect of Christian worship finds expression in various forms. The public reading of God's Word is one. God's Word comes to us from outside, confronts us with God's revelation, and challenges all human attempts to reach him by human effort or to remake him in human image. When the Word is read in the congregation, the claims of the world (whether the wider world "out there" or the inner world within ourselves) are repudiated and the claims of God are asserted in opposition to them.

Singing praise to God is another area of countercultural rebellion in the worship service. The world around us cries out to have our worship, the devotion of our hearts, to be praised by us for what it is and what it can do. Singing praise to God is denying praise to the world and thus denying the world's claims upon us.

Corporate reading of a creed or confession is a third aspect of this kind of rebellion. Because the great creeds and confessions summarize so wonderfully important aspects of the Bible's teaching, not least the sovereign kingship of God, which relativizes the claims to kingship of all creatures, their recitation is an act of defiance and an insult to creaturely arrivistes. As soon as the congregation says "We believe in one God . . ." all other pretenders to the divine throne have been put well and truly in their place. Neither sex nor money nor power is God; there is only one God, the God whom the creed proceeds to describe.

Far from being a staid piece of outmoded traditionalism, such a corporate action is a devastating blow against the cultural conformity that demands the church be just like the world, accept the same criteria of relevance, truth, and aesthetics as the world, and offer a gospel that accommodates at least some of the claims of the world. The recitation of a creed makes it very clear that, whatever the attitude of heart of any individual church member, the church as a whole looks to God as king, not some creaturely pretender.

Creeds Ascribe to God What Belongs to Him and Him Alone

Third, and more briefly as it is basically part of the first two points, creeds ascribe to God what belongs to him and to him alone. It is of the nature of us as fallen human beings to forget who God is, to remake him in our own image, and to domesticate him in such a way that he conforms to the limited dimensions of our own imaginations. We go to church each week in part to be reminded by that Word which comes from outside of us who God is, what he has done, and what he will do. The corporate recitation of a creed forces us to engage in the positive action of ascribing to him that which is his: the glories of his nature; the marvelous details of his actions; and the great promise of the future consummation of the kingdom. That is worship: giving to God what is his.

In this context, it is hard to understand why any church that uses hymns or choruses or any song that has been written beforehand and is sung in unison by everyone present would object to reciting a creed. Hymn singing is only corporate recitation set to music; and no hymns of which I am aware consistently contain as much sound theology per clause as the Apostles' or Nicene Creeds. Is it thus the lack of musical accompaniment which makes churches wary of the use of creeds? Well, there are musical arrangements for such, though, ironically, use of such is often suspected by anticreedal churches of indicating Roman Catholic tendencies. So, if it is not the music, what is it? It cannot be an objection to the words; in all likelihood, it is simply a judgment based on taste, whereby the pastor or elders or congregation do not like to recite creeds because it just feels a bit too Romish for their liking. Such an objection is unworthy of the expenditure of time to refute any further than I have already done in these chapters.

Conclusion

Those who object to the use of creedal material in Christian praise typically do so for a variety of reasons: forms of words lead to mere formalism in worship; preaching on a catechism is not preaching on the Bible; speaking human words in the worship service supplants the unique authority of Scripture.

As we have noted, these are all specious objections. All churches have forms of words which they use, typically hymns or choruses. Preaching on a catechism simply provides a framework for making sure that all of the major biblical doctrines are covered within a set period of time. As to speaking human words in a worship service, virtually every word spoken there is a human word, with the exception of the passages of Scripture that are read out loud (and even then, these are typically translations of God's word, not God's word in and of itself).

In addition, I would argue that if one takes Scripture seriously and sees it as regulating both the form, content, and purpose of Christian praise, then it is hard to see why creedal material should not be included in the service. Scripture uses forms, of which the Psalms are the most obvious. The content of praise is an accurate account of who God is and what he has done. The purpose of praise is to ascribe to him what belongs to him alone. It is hard to see how this can be done more effectively and indeed concisely than through the use of creeds in the worship service. They are no more human intrusions into worship than are extemporary prayers. The one big difference is that an orthodox creed contains no unpleasant surprises in the form of heterodox or even heretical theology, embarrassing phraseology, inappropriate childishness, or personal idiosyncrasies and obsessions. Tried and tested over the years, the best creeds contain solid theology clearly expressed in appropriate language. The question is not so much "Should we use them?" as "Why would we not use them?" They do nothing but ensure that biblical content and priorities are kept uppermost in the public worship of the church.

6

On the Usefulness of Creeds and Confessions

The main burden of this book thus far has been to argue that creeds and confessions are not simply consistent with biblical teaching but that their existence and use are even strongly implied by the same; and also that the history of the church demonstrates that they have frequently been of great help in the maintenance and propagation of the Christian faith. Now, in this last chapter, I want to conclude by listing a series of further advantages that the church can enjoy if she gives creeds and confessions their proper place in her daily life. The list is not exhaustive, and many readers may well think of others they might wish to add or, perhaps, of ones I list which they would exclude on the grounds that some other thing might do the task even more effectively. Thus, I offer this as no definitive list, nor do I present these ideas in order of priority, preference, or importance. I merely hope that they will stimulate the reader to further constructive reflection upon the creedal imperative of the church.

All Churches and All Christians Have Creeds and Confessions

The first point I want to make in this concluding chapter is one that has been mentioned on a couple of occasions throughout the book and has perhaps frequently lurked below the surface elsewhere: all churches and all Christians have a creed or a confession. What I mean by this is that no church or Christian simply believes the Bible. The Bible in itself is a collection of various genres of literature. I believe it ultimately communicates a coherent message, but no Christian, if asked by a friend what the Bible teaches, is simply going to start reading aloud at Genesis 1:1 and not stop until Revelation 22:21. Instead, when asked by friends what the Bible teaches, we all try to offer a synthesis, a summary of what the Bible says. And as we move from biblical text to theological statement, we offer what is, in terms of content, something akin to a creed or confession. Then, if we reflect honestly on how we read the Bible, we will acknowledge that what we think the Bible teaches as a whole will shape how we understand individual verses, chapters, and books.

Given this, we need not take too seriously those who claim to have no creed but the Bible. If this is intended in the sense that "we have no ultimate authority for norming theological statements other than the Bible," then conservative Protestant Christians would generally all agree. If, however, it is intended in the sense that I have no understanding of the Bible other than the Bible itself, then that is highly misleading. The character I mentioned in the opening paragraphs of the introduction claimed no creed but the Bible, yet he was dispensationalist in eschatology, Calvinist in soteriology, and brethren in ecclesiology. What he really should have said was: I have a creed but I am not going to write it down, so you cannot critique it; and I am going to identify my creed so closely with the Bible that I am not going to be able to critique it either.

There are numerous obvious ironies here, not least that last point. It is probable this person objected to creeds on the grounds that they represent a man-made framework which was imposed upon the Bible by the church and thus distorted how the Bible was read. In fact, by refusing to acknowledge even the existence of his own framework, he removed any possibility of assessing that framework in the light of Scripture. Thus, he invested more absolute authority in his private creed and his tradition than even the Roman Catholic Church or the Eastern Orthodox, who at least have the decency to put their confessional standards into the public domain.

The standard evangelical objection to creeds and confessions is simply not sustainable in the light of its own self-referential incoherence, the Bible's own teaching, and the history of the church. I argued in an earlier chapter that creeds and confessions actually fulfill a vital role in a function that Paul makes an imperative for the church and her leadership, that of the stable transmission of the gospel from one generation to another. Thus, if you take the Bible seriously, you will either have a creed or a confession or something that fulfills the same basic role, such as a statement of faith. Here, I want to make the point that those who repudiate such ideas are being unintentionally disingenuous: they still have their creed or confession; they just will not write it down and allow you to look at it and scrutinize it in the light of Scripture. They are in a sense more authoritarian than the papacy.

In fact, a church which is open about its confessional position is, in theory at least, better able to do justice to the supreme authority of Scripture. First, to repeat, the use of a confession is consistent with the Bible's own teaching and actually addresses a matter that the Bible makes an imperative. Second, once the creed or confession is in the public domain, mechanisms can be put in place to allow for it to function in a subordinate role to Scripture.[1]

To achieve this, a confession is not enough. The church also needs mechanisms to ensure that, on the one hand, the confession does not become an unassailable idol and, on the other hand, that it is not subject to the arbitrary wild interpretation. No system can do this perfectly: the church, by definition, is made up of sinful failures and that capacity for failure and sin continues throughout our church lives. Yet a church that is open about its confessional commitments

---

[1]Hermeneutical skeptics will object here that the introduction of a creed or confession does not solve the problem of interpretation: as the Bible needs to be interpreted, so do creeds and confessions. Thus, one could end up with an infinite regression of interpretations or, to use the trendier jargon, an endless deferral of meaning. This is not the place to discuss whether texts have meanings. For that, I would refer interested readers to Kevin J. Vanhoozer, *Is There a Meaning in This Text?* (Leicester, UK: Apollos, 1998). Suffice it to say here that, assuming texts do have meanings, it seems clear that some texts are easier to interpret than others; and creeds and confessions are designed to offer clear and succinct statements of faith. That debates can and do rage over points of interpretation relative to these documents is undeniable; but that the scope of these debates is considerably narrower than those which rage around the Bible is also undeniable.

and that strives to maintain a structure of governance which reflects biblical concepts of eldership is inevitably better placed to negotiate the relationship between Scripture and confession than the church which lacks these things.

In confessional Presbyterianism, the church typically requires all office-bearers to profess belief in the system of doctrine as expressed in the Westminster Standards, to uphold the teaching thereof, and to register any change of mind with the relevant body.[2] The purpose of this is to ensure that the church knows what is being taught from her pulpits and promulgated by her office-bearers. Thus, for example, if a minister in a Presbyterian church were to become convinced that infant baptism was not biblical, he would be required to report that change to his presbytery and would be asked to demit the office. This does not mean that the church no longer considers him to be a Christian, but simply that, while she respects his conscience on this matter, integrity requires that she no longer allow him to hold office within the ranks of a Presbyterian church. The church's position and the action relative to the minister who has changed his mind would both be matters of public record. Nobody could claim that the church had acted inappropriately. The same, of course, would be true in a Baptist church where the minister became convinced of paedobaptism. It would scarcely be unfair for the elder board to ask him to step down. What would be disingenuous in both cases would be for a church to claim to hold to a certain confessional position on baptism and yet allow someone taking the opposite view to hold ministerial office.

Imagine, however, a church that has "no creed but the Bible," where the minister one week is convinced that baptism should be restricted only to professing believers and the next week changes his mind and thinks babies can be baptized too. Can he be held to account? There would seem to be no way of doing this; in practice, whatever he thinks is the truth on any given matter at any given moment—that is the position of his church. This is surely a recipe for chaos in that it places the congregation completely at the mercy of whatever the current

---

[2]For the local church elder, that would be the session, or elder board, of the local church; for a minister, that would the presbytery, or regional body made up of ministers and representative elders from each congregation.

opinion of the pastor might be. He has, in theory, unlimited power, and the Bible would seem to mean whatever he decides that it means.

Imagine, too, a church whose confession teaches that salvation comes about by the free will of human beings and that God only looks on hopefully, trying to establish favorable conditions for conversions but having no decisive say in the matter. Let us say that a majority of her people and office-bearers at some point come to the conclusion that this is incorrect, that the confessional document to which they hold needs to be revised on this point. A church with an established process by which this change can be accomplished can do this in a manner that is public, transparent, and which involves wrestling with Scripture's teaching in a corporate context. Such a procedure would not simply allow the church's ministers to stand up one Sunday and teach whatever they wanted on the topic.[3] That would lead to anarchy and confusion. Yet a church where the minister "has no creed but the Bible" can have no transparent mechanism for effecting the change. What the minister believes and what the Bible teaches are functionally identified. If he thinks it teaches Pelagianism one Sunday and Calvinism the next, who is to contradict him and how could they do so? Again, the congregation is at the mercy of the minister.

Thus, one obvious advantage of having an open, public confession is that it makes transparent that which is practically hidden by evangelical claims to having no creed but the Bible: everybody has a creed; the only difference is whether you are prepared to be honest and open about that fact. Further, only once you have acknowledged this and made your creed public can you then put into place a system that connects your church's confession to Scripture and to the church's government in a way that gives your church, her leadership, and her people a way of making sure that the confession stays subordinate to Scripture in a transparent, orderly, and public way. Ironically, it is not the confessionalists but the "no creed but the Bible" people who exalt their creeds above Scripture.

Confessions Delimit the Power of the Church

Closely related to the last point, and one that is often missed, is that confessions serve to delimit the power of the church and of her office-

---

[3] I deal with the matter of confessional revision in the appendix.

bearers. This is somewhat counterintuitive in an age which is typically very suspicious of anything that smacks of institutional authority, and where there is a church culture that often sees creedal documents as blunt instruments for excluding some and manipulating others. Yet this is possibly one of the most important functions confessional documents can fulfill.

We have noted two important aspects of eldership: doctrinal competence and authority. The two things are linked, and it is clear that, practically speaking, the nature of that linkage is crucial. Doctrinal competence without authority renders the office impotent and prevents the elders from leading a congregation toward spiritual maturity. Authority without doctrinal competence, however, is a recipe for willful despotism, where the church is whatever the elders decide, no more and no less. Indeed, the history of religion is full of sad stories of church leaders who used their power over their followers to perpetrate terrible tragedies. From Münster in the Reformation to Jonestown and beyond, charismatic figures have used religion to control and manipulate people. Certainty in religion can easily lead to disaster; thus, it is crucial for churches to reflect upon exactly what it is that they are and what powers they do and do not have.

In order to establish church power within appropriate limits, several things need to be in place. First, there needs to be a clear understanding of what the church is. Second, and flowing from the first, there needs to be a statement of the church's beliefs, that is, a confession of faith. Third, there needs to be a set of procedures that articulate and define how the confession of faith is to be practically applied within the congregation. It is the role of the first and second of these which are obviously of concern to us here.

In any institution or organization with a hierarchical structure, central to its well-being will be the organization's own understanding of its purpose, and the acceptance of this by its members or employees. For example, I worked for some years as Academic Dean at a theological seminary. This particular seminary has three stated purposes: to train men for ordained ministry; to train men and women for nonordained leadership roles within the broader Christian world; and to train potential future scholars. If I thus entered the classroom one day and started teaching my students about one of my personal passions—say, long-distance running or how to watch a rugby game or the Tour de France—my students would be rightfully displeased because they have paid the institution money in order to be trained by me in church history, not sporting fixtures. To lodge their complaint successfully, the students would need only to point to the seminary's own description of its mission in order to establish that something had gone wrong in the Trueman classroom.

A confession functions in an analogous way for the church: it describes the message which the church is to preach, and it limits the church's power to what is contained within that document. Take, for example, a minister who decides that the Bible teaches that all Christians should wear clothes of a certain style. Such a case might be bizarre, but how would the church where the minister has "no creed but the Bible" handle this situation? Hermeneutical issues and church power issues would combine in a most awkward manner.

Of course, while certain churches do seem to encourage a certain aesthetic when it comes to dress, there are probably very few where the eldership engage in an explicit and high-handed approach to congregants' fashion sense. More likely in the current climate will be an eldership that issues edicts about where one should send one's children to school, for whom one should vote, whether couples should use contraception and even, in some case, the specific person one should marry. Some of these issues are more debatable than others but all represent a direct intrusion of the church into areas of life which, generally speaking, are not matters in which the church should directly concern itself.[4]

When one looks at the New Testament, it is interesting to see that Paul has to address issues of the abuse of church power on numerous occasions. For example, in Galatians 5:12–13, Paul warns against those who are insisting that the Galatians need to be circumcised. This is typically (and correctly) understood as Paul attacking attempts by

---

[4] I am aware that some issues, such as contraception and education, are increasingly contentious. I do not wish to engage the specifics of these matters in this book; my interest here is whether the church has the right to issue specific edicts in these areas rather than simply inculcating general principles that leave the individual free to make appropriate applications in his or her family or private lives.

"Judaizers" to pull the church back into Jewish practices because they have not understood the full implications of the gospel. That is true; but it is also an example of Paul attacking the illegitimate extension of church power. The New Testament church's power is delimited by the gospel. Thus, for church leaders to insist on the necessary addition of anything, be it circumcision, ceremonial washings, or whatever, is for them to step beyond any power that God has given the church. We see a similar situation in the letter to the Colossians, where Paul advises the people to let no one judge them with regard to observance of peripheral things such as food, festivals, or Sabbaths. Again, the subtext is not just that a form of legalism had crept in to the church at Colossae; it also appears that this was connected to a dictatorial church eldership, as is typically the case in such situations.

In these contexts, confessions can be remarkably helpful. As they offer succinct summaries of doctrine, so they also offer succinct summaries of what can be expected of the Christian in terms of practice. It is true that Paul did not have a confession in the sense that we can now have one, but that is not the question to ask. The question is one of what mechanisms are best to maintain the kind of church envisaged by Paul in the early church. How do we create a church community where what is regarded as normal belief and practice is publicly stated in such a fashion that it expresses biblical teaching, can be challenged and tested in the light of Scripture, and allows both elders and laypeople to know exactly where they stand in relationship to each other? A public, church-sanctioned confession is the obvious answer; it may, of course, not be the only answer, but it seems to me to be the best. If the wheel does the job reasonably well, why would one wish to reinvent it?

Thus, in the church where I am on session, I am aware that if I stand up one Sunday and declare that I am going to discipline all members who do not homeschool their children or vote for the Libertarian Party or throw away their television sets or start using homoeopathic medicine or give up drinking alcohol, the congregation can legitimately ask me where it says they need to do that according to the church's stated public position in her confessions. To put it bluntly, the members did not sign up for this and I therefore have no right to require it of them.

For the church where there is "no creed but the Bible," however, the situation is likely to be much more complicated and rapidly become very messy. This is not to deny that such a church might possibly achieve the correct result at some point, but the process will be much murkier and much more open to abuse and misreading than if there is a clearly stated summary of biblical teaching in the form of a confession to which the congregation can have recourse. Just as a good civil law code defines a well-ordered society and the powers its various estates possess, a confession states clearly that for which a church stands and thus allows the people to know what to expect from the eldership and, most importantly, when the eldership is overstepping its bounds. Of course, a confession is no guarantee that abuse of power will not take place, but it is one important element of a framework for making such less likely. Good confessions properly applied by appropriately qualified and ordained elders do actually hinder despotic church power and protect the members; they do not facilitate it.

Creeds and Confessions Offer Succinct and Thorough Summaries of the Faith

Once one has acknowledged that every church has a creed and that, for good order, such a creed needs to be publicly stated, it becomes clear that there are numerous further advantages to this. Of these, perhaps the most obvious is not particularly ecclesiastical: they offer more comprehensive and succinct summaries of Christian doctrine than anything else. Indeed, one might without hyperbole declare that, outside of the Bible, the documents that contain more biblical truth per page than anything else are the great creeds and confessions of the church. It is worth noting two related aspects of this as being of use to the church: first, they focus the church's mind on the main thing; second, they remind us that "succinctness" in Christian theology is not necessarily what our contemporary culture tells us that it is.

First, creeds and confessions focus the church's mind on the main thing. Longevity is one of the great assets that the church's creedal statements have in their favor: they were produced long ago and have withstood the test of time. While that is not in and of itself a watertight argument for their authority, it does at least indicate that the topics they address are clearly the hardy perennials of Christian existence. We shall comment later that one of the great advantages of such is that they relativize the present; here we should note that the classic confessions of the church, for all of their doctrinal differences, focus on matters such as the doctrines of God, of creation, of Christ, of redemption, of salvation, and of consummation. A church with a creed or confession has a built-in gospel reality check. It is unlikely to become sidetracked by the peripheral issues of the passing moment; rather it will focus instead on the great theological categories that touch on matters of eternal significance.

The second factor is the succinctness of creeds and confessions. Of course, we live in an age where numerous factors militate against considering the classical confessions as succinct summaries. We noted in chapter 1 the woeful influence of things like Wikipedia in leading some to think that all important knowledge can be swiftly grasped in short sentences and after a few minutes of cursory reading. Further, the role of the evangelical parachurch today, which depends upon the sidelining of many traditional confessional topics such as sacraments, means that the kind of statements of faith and doctrinal bases with which many are familiar are often ten or twelve point documents that can be easily printed on a single sheet of paper. Notions of what is "succinct" have somewhat contracted over the years. When one considers that the Shorter Catechism of the Westminster Assembly, amounting to 107 brief questions and answers, was really the elementary pedagogical document that simply prepared the way for the main event, the Larger Catechism of 196 far more elaborate questions, one realizes that what does and does not constitute the bare essentials of a coherent faith has certainly changed since the seventeenth century. Few even among Presbyterians today know the Shorter Catechism by heart, let alone the Larger.

We need to hold this in mind when we hear the oft-repeated complaints about creeds and confessions, particularly the more elaborate productions of the sixteenth and seventeenth centuries such as the Belgic and the Westminster, that they are so elaborate and prescriptive. One of the points that must be made in response to such criticism is that these documents typically cover only the really basic heads of Christian doctrine. Take Westminster as an example: would one really want to have a church confession that said nothing about the doctrine of Scripture, the doctrine of God, the nature of justification and sanctification, the definition of the church, and so on? One might dissent from the content of such topics in the Confession but one could scarcely argue that they did not represent some of the most basic concerns of the Bible itself.

In fact, many churches do have statements which do not touch on these issues explicitly, and one must then ask: is the document to which they do subscribe sufficient to give the elders the necessary material with which to maintain as far as possible the orthodoxy of the church?

Any church needs to avoid two things in this context. First, the church must not send the signal that things which are actually important are matters of indifference. Here one needs to be careful of making one's own issues into *the* issues (something that the relativizing effect of creeds can help with, as will be argued below). Just because the current elders think that, say, wearing a dark suit in the pulpit is appropriate for preachers does not mean that this should necessarily be part of the church's confessional documents. It is still the case, however, that there are matters about which Scripture speaks eloquently and which must therefore feature in any church's confession. Baptism is perhaps the most obvious. There is extensive biblical teaching on this issue, and both the New Testament narratives of the Gospels and Acts and the teaching of Paul in his Letters makes it clear this is not a topic one can simply ignore. Thus, for a church to have a statement of faith that does not articulate a specific position on this matter would appear to be at odds with what is indisputable: the importance of the topic for the church of the New Testament. Indeed, I would argue that the church which sees the issue is of great importance, whatever the conclusion about its mode and subjects, is more consistent with New Testament emphases than the one which ignores the matter in its confessional statement or simply leaves it up to the conscience of the individual. A confessional document needs to reflect the doctrinal emphases and priorities of Scripture.[5]

---

[5]This is again where church history becomes important because it allows access to what has been considered important throughout the ages and not simply within the narrow confines of the my own present time.

The second issue is that, for a church to maintain a consistently orthodox witness, a certain level of ineradicable complexity is necessary in her doctrinal statements in order for them to be theologically stable. In this, the church's doctrinal confession is analogous to the nature of living organisms. If you drop below a certain level of complexity—genetic, physiological, or whatever—life becomes simply unsustainable. As a mouse needs a heart, blood, a brain, teeth, a digestive system, etc., and a genetic makeup that provides all the above or else it will perish, so a church confession needs a level of complexity in order for each of its doctrines to be stable and to function correctly within her life.

The history of doctrine bears ample witness to this fact. Think, for example, of the incarnation of the Son in the person of the Lord Jesus Christ. To maintain this, one needs not only a grasp of what deity is and what humanity is, one must also have a Trinitarian understanding of God, otherwise one falls off the ridge into either modalism on the one side or tritheism on the other. Thus, any confessional document that talks about the incarnation must also talk about the Trinity. This is why a study of the development of doctrinal statements in church history is important: it gives a first-rate insight into how doctrines interconnect and how formulations that solve one set of questions then create the ground for a new set. Chalcedon was only possible in the light of Nicaea; but once Nicaea was in place, Chalcedon, or some equivalent, became necessary as a means of connecting the dots from God in himself to God manifest in the flesh.

One might also say a similar thing about justification. Justification connects to one's understanding of humanity, of sin, of Christ's person and work, of faith, and of final judgment. One cannot simply put forward a church statement that declares, "We believe in justification by faith." It is arguable that some Roman Catholics would be able to interpret that statement in a manner consistent with their own catechism. To be distinctly Protestant, one has to provide much more detail and set this doctrine within a complex of other doctrines. One needs to define God, creation, God's image, the impact of the fall, the nature of righteousness, and what constitutes faith, imputation, etc. A doctrine of justification is only stable once it is set within a broader doctrinal matrix.

This is perhaps an odd direction for the argument to take in a section that recommends confessions as *succinct* summaries of the faith, but as I noted above, the notion of what is and is not *succinct* has rather changed over the years; and we need to allow our understanding of it to be shaped by the Bible and by how the thought of the Bible has been articulated over the ages in church documents. Succinct means neither longer nor shorter than necessary. The promulgation (and, where necessary, the defense) of orthodoxy is massively enhanced by an adequately complex confession because such a document helps strengthen ecclesiology.

Furthermore, from the point of view of basic pedagogy, it is surely to the church's advantage to have a creed or confession. If you want to offer a curriculum on what is important in the Bible, it is useful to have a brief syllabus that encompasses all the key points. A good confession will do that. Plus, if you yourself want a book that you can carry in your pocket which will serve as a reminder of the grand sweep of biblical teaching, then you want to obtain a copy of a confession and carry it with you always.

This is not, of course, to argue that the Westminster Confession, or the alternatives, offers an exhaustive account of everything that the Bible teaches. Far from it. But it is to say that it will provide reasonable coverage of the basic essentials.

Creeds and Confessions Allow for Appropriate Discrimination between Members and Office-Bearers

One of the things with which we need to take special care in the use of creeds and confessions by the church is the function these have for non-office-bearing members. Should laypeople be required to subscribe to a church's doctrinal standards in the same way as an elder or a deacon? Some traditions, for example a number of the continental Reformed churches, have a history of requiring confessional subscription of every communicant member. This is a complex issue and worthy of full-orbed discussion; here, however, I wish to present not a polemic against such a view but a positive exposition of the standard Presbyterian position. This position is the one which I will argue fits best with the biblical evidence and can also be applied to other church polities.

In Presbyterianism, an important function of creeds and confessions is the way in which they allow for an appropriate distinction between the qualifications for membership and those for office-bearing. This is something that I believe Presbyterianism (at least in theory—always an important qualification when it comes to ecclesiology) actually does well. Typically, Presbyterians set the bar for full communicant church membership very low: a simple but publicly coherent profession of faith in the line of Romans 10:9–10 is sufficient. This may be fleshed out in a series of simple vows, touching on issues such as the Trinity, salvation by grace through faith, the authority of the Bible, and submission to elder oversight, but the overall content is simple and straightforward. Many Presbyterian churches also require individuals to participate in a series of membership classes that elaborate this basic profession and also instruct candidates about the seriousness of the commitment which membership involves. But the basic criteria are the simple ones of Romans 10: a basic trust in Christ and an outward profession which is consistent with that. It is surely important, and consistent with a view of God as merciful and gracious, that we set the bar for membership no higher than that which we find in the Bible itself.

For example, it would seem to me to be inappropriate that people be required to finely parse the communication of attributes in the person of Christ prior to becoming a member of a church. Similarly, it is surely unreasonable for them to be required to articulate and resolve the many problems that initially arise out of the confession that God is three and God is one. These are things that the church is to teach to her members, not require of them prior to entry. Indeed, if fulsome knowledge of the whole counsel of God were required for mere membership, one might be left wondering exactly what it is that the church is supposed to do with those who finally manage to join. Membership is not a reward for achieving a high level of doctrinal knowledge any more than a high level of personal holiness. It is the gateway to the means by which these things can become possible via the ordinary means of grace.

Nevertheless, the Bible makes it quite clear that qualifications for office-bearing are of a somewhat different order. Thus, in 1 Timothy Paul starts the letter by stressing to Timothy the nature of his charge as elder:

Paul, an apostle of Christ Jesus by command of God our Savior and of Christ Jesus our hope, To Timothy, my true child in the faith: Grace, mercy, and peace from God the Father and Christ Jesus our Lord. As I urged you when I was going to Macedonia, remain at Ephesus that you may charge certain persons not to teach any different doctrine, nor to devote themselves to myths and endless genealogies, which promote speculations rather than the stewardship from God that is by faith. The aim of our charge is love that issues from a pure heart and a good conscience and a sincere faith. Certain persons, by swerving from these, have wandered away into vain discussion, desiring to be teachers of the law, without understanding either what they are saying or the things about which they make confident assertions.

It is clear from this that Paul sees Timothy's task as elder as involving the careful communication of the faith in a manner that focuses on the straightforward teaching of the gospel. The elder is to do this by avoiding the kind of undoubtedly fascinating but ultimately sterile obsession with elaborate speculations that mark these problem figures at Ephesus. In other words, he is to have the maturity and discernment to know what exactly it is that he is to focus on in terms of his teaching, and the knowledge to be able to do this effectively. He is also to make sure that his ambition is to teach, not to be a teacher. This might seem a small point but ultimately touches on a crucial aspect of attitude: the teacher's task is to draw attention to what is taught, not to himself.

Given this, it is clear that Paul assumes that the teacher is to have a certain doctrinal competence which may not typically mark the church member. After all, if the church members all possessed this competence, there would presumably be no such problem as Paul describes in Ephesus. Thus, later in the same letter Paul outlines the qualities of an elder in a more elaborate fashion, essentially making explicit some of the aspects implied in his initial exhortation to Timothy:

The saying is trustworthy: If anyone aspires to the office of overseer, he desires a noble task. Therefore an overseer must be above reproach, the husband of one wife, sober-minded, self-controlled, respectable, hospitable, able to teach, not a drunkard, not violent but gentle, not quarrelsome, not a lover of money. He must manage his own household well, with all dignity keeping his children submissive, for if someone does not know how to manage his own household, how will he care for God's church? He must not be a recent convert, or he may become puffed up with conceit and fall into the condemnation of the devil. Moreover, he must be well thought of by outsiders, so that he may not fall into disgrace, into a snare of the devil. (1 Tim. 3:1–7)

While it is helpful to note that doctrinal qualifications are only one of the many things Paul lists as necessary for an elder, in the context of this chapter it is important to stress that the ability to teach is non-negotiable and clearly carries with it significant doctrinal freight. For Paul, one cannot be a teacher in the abstract: what one teaches, the content, is a vital part of the task; one can only be a teacher when one has sufficient mastery of this appropriate content to be able to teach it.

The question for each individual church or denomination becomes, therefore, what is it that the elders are to be competent to teach? What content is it that they are supposed to have sufficiently mastered in order to hold this office? What more do they need to believe and to understand than the teenager who was converted last Sunday morning on his first visit to the church?

A couple of answers might immediately suggest themselves. One could respond simply: the deep things of the Bible. This idea, however, is vulnerable to precisely the kind of problem noted earlier about a church simply holding to the Bible as its standard of orthodoxy. Every heretic has his text. The pastor who simply declares that his creed is the Bible and nothing more is being disingenuous because, when he preaches, he interprets the Bible, he does not simply read it aloud to his congregation. And if he decides the text means one thing this week and the opposite the next, how can the congregation hold him to account for what he is teaching? Further, we might also recall the argument above about the delimiting of church power. If the pastor is simply "teaching the Bible," and there is no frame of reference by which the congregation can assess that teaching, then the possibility for abuse of power becomes much more real.

If your church has a minimal doctrinal basis or statement, however, the response might be that elders should be free to teach whatever they consider to be consistent with Scripture, which is also consistent with the doctrinal basis. This is plausible but points us to the problem noted above, that Christian theology has a certain ineradicable complexity whereby certain doctrines stand in positive connection to others, and where modification of one might well require modification of another. This is not to say that simple childlike faith that Jesus is Lord is not sufficient for salvation; but it is to say that this is insufficient for the establishment and well-being of the church as a community which confesses the same. We noted in chapter 2 that the New Testament envisages the church as a place where people grow, and one aspect of that growth that is explicitly mentioned is increase in knowledge; and requiring elders to be committed to a confession of faith is a means of trying to ensure that those in positions of teaching authority have the knowledge and the ability to foster that growth among the congregation. Indeed, the church that can only regulate the teaching that it permits in a minimal way is never going to rise above that minimal level when it comes to coherent public, doctrinal testimony, something implicit in the previous point.

For this reason, those who take the New Testament teaching on the church and on the eldership seriously need to put in place mechanisms that allow that teaching to be realized in practice. The most obvious way of doing this is to require elders to subscribe to a confession of faith that articulates the kind of doctrinal complexity which is necessary for the elaboration and defense of the central tenets of the faith. Doing so holds such men accountable for what they believe and teach; yet restricting this to the eldership (and in many cases the diaconate) allows for the setting of an appropriately different level for members. It recognizes the seriousness of the office of elder but also the fact that many genuine believers have minimal doctrinal understanding at their conversion. It allows that this should not be a bar to church membership—membership which then provides the context for their growth in this area as in others.

Creeds and Confessions Reflect the Ministerial Authority of the Church

One of the most important aspects of creeds and confessions is that they are corporate documents which are authored and owned by the corporate churches, as represented by her office-bearers. We noted in both chapter 2 and earlier in this chapter that Paul puts particular weight upon the eldership, both in terms of its responsibility to safeguard the orthodoxy of the church's public proclamation of the gospel, and of the authority it therefore has to make sure this is done.

Now, creeds and confessions can, historically, be the work of a single hand. The Belgic Confession is one good example; the Heidelberg Catechism is another. Yet both of these documents have status not because of who wrote them but because duly appointed church officers have formally adopted them as confessional standards, for regulating teaching and preaching. They thus become corporate church documents, not simply the private musings of gifted theologians.

As Protestants, we are of course naturally wary of any kind of claims for church authority that would place the church over Scripture or exhibit the kind of sacerdotal or papal tendencies we associate with Roman Catholicism. Nevertheless, Paul does have an ecclesiology whereby specially qualified and elected men hold the office of elder, and that office involves both authority and responsibility.

In this context, members of churches are to take very seriously creeds and confessions, not simply where they think the teaching they contain coincides with Scripture, but because they are upheld by the elders of the church, who, as Paul tells us, are worthy of respect and to whom we should submit in the Lord. This can be a delicate balance: the elders are not part of an unassailable hierarchy that must be uncritically obeyed in all matters, but nor are they to be treated as just anybody else in the church. One might say they are analogous to schoolteachers or policemen: their status does not automatically guarantee that they will always act correctly or that they should be unconditionally obeyed simply because of who they are, but ninety-nine times out of a hundred, their status should be significant in determining our response to them.

Thus it is with creeds and confessions. Because these documents have been adopted by those who have been called to hold office in Christ's church—and that carries huge weight in and of itself—the default position should be one of trust and obedience toward them. No, this does not mean that, unlike the Bereans, we should not search the Scriptures to see if the things they claim are so. But it does mean we should be less confident of our judgment and more inclined to trust the church, an attitude which clearly goes against our current cultural predilection toward suspicion and iconoclasm.

It is perhaps very hard, particularly for Protestants, to think in such terms today. Those of us in the West have been taught to believe so deeply in the authority and autonomy of the individual that subjecting our own thoughts to external authorities, especially corporate or historic, is very counterintuitive. Combined with a desire for instant gratification, many of us are inclined to believe that if something does not make sense the first time we look at it, it—and not we—must be wrong. That is not the way the church operates. It is clear in the New Testament that the corporate nature of the church is important in terms of practice and belief; the history and nature of confessions witness to that and connect it to the officers of the church as well.

Paul has a high view of the church as a body and as an institution. This has been reflected, sometimes excessively so, in church history from Ignatius onward. Yet the fact remains that respect for the authority of the church and respect for the creeds and confessions which churches adopt must become an important part of our contemporary Christian lives if we are to be truly biblical. That society tells us to distrust traditional authority, to doubt all leaders, and to dismiss the past is of little relevance to applying biblical principles to our churches.

Creeds and Confessions Represent the Maximum Doctrinal Competence That Can Be Expected from a Congregation

Underlying the last point is the notion that creeds and confessions can also have an important pedagogical function within the church. As we noted above, they are succinct doctrinal summaries. They also represent that which the church aspires to teach its members, and that is why confessional churches typically have at least one catechism among their subordinate standards. In short, they represent the church's doctrinal and pedagogical aspirations.

We can make this point by reflecting for a moment on the function of law codes in society at large. Many countries have laws that its citizens know will be broken. A recent controversial example would be that of the torture of terrorist suspects. This led some in the USA to suggest that it might be desirable to change the law. Should torture be legalized and thus be subject to regulation? Or should it be kept illegal, even though it is tacitly understood that the law will on occasion be broken? Both arguments have a certain power, but my own instincts incline me to the latter position for the simple reason that laws represent in part the moral aspirations of a given society. Nobody, for example, believes that outlawing abortion will stop abortion; but many of us would wish to live in a society where the statute books represent our aspiration to be an abortion-free society. That is one reason we want it to be illegal: laws set before us a vision of the kind of society we would like to see realized. They do not simply reflect the pragmatic reality which we all know.

There is an analogy here with the churchly nature of creeds and confessions. For a church to hold to a creed or confession, to require subscription to the same from her office-bearers, is to send a signal to the congregation about what the church considers to be important in her doctrinal life. If a church has a six-point creed or confession, she essentially communicates to her people that these six things, and only these, are important. Everything else is so minor that it forms no part of its identity and it is quite happy for anything to be taught on other topics providing that such teaching does not come into direct conflict with the six basic points.

On one level, setting the bar this low is commendable in that it reflects the fact that church membership should require no more doctrinal competence than that which the Bible specifies for salvation. We do not want to stop new converts from coming into church membership and under the pastoral care of a local congregation because they do not yet understand the hypostatic union of the two natures in Christ or have not fully developed a theology of the Trinity. We also do not want to exclude from membership the educationally challenged or those who cannot think abstractly and are never going to be able to articulate a clear defense of the Chalcedonian Definition. We want church membership to be as inclusive as the Bible makes it. Nevertheless, we surely do not want to send a signal to the congregation that members should simply be satisfied with a basic, mere Christianity, especially since the Bible itself clearly sets an ambitious standard for doctrinal understanding and expects growth in such understanding to be a normal result of belonging to the church. After all, Paul himself is able to distinguish between the kind of basic teaching given to new believers and the more sophisticated ideas to which such believers should progress. Membership is the beginning, not the end, of the pedagogical process.

Given this, a church confession not only sets before the congregation a list of doctrinal priorities and demonstrates how these priorities fit together into an overarching framework, it also represents an aspirational ideal of what the eldership hopes will be the appropriate level of doctrinal competence for the congregation. If something is a priority, is of importance, then it should be stated in the confession. If it is not in the confession, then it will be very hard to make the case that it is of any importance. After all, if one does not need to have an opinion on a topic to hold office, then that topic is clearly of highly negotiable significance.

An obvious example here would be baptism. If the confessional statement takes no stand on baptism and does not make it clear if it is to be applied to believers only or to believers and their children, the obvious conclusion is that baptism is of no real significance, that the church has no more need to have an opinion on this matter than on what color wallpaper will be best for the fellowship hall. Yet it is surely very difficult to square any notion of baptism as a matter indifferent with the frequent and vigorous teaching of Paul on the matter in the New Testament.

That confessions also delimit the power of the church also reinforces the notion that a church's confession really sets forth the maximum level of theological understanding that can be normatively required from members. This is not to say that individual members cannot and will not deepen their theological knowledge in ways untouched by the confession. Indeed, it should be the hope of every church that the membership will be as theologically well-read and literate as possible. Nevertheless, as the confession sets out what the church considers to be vital, and also sets the material parameters of the church's pedagogical power, we must understand that it represents the maximum that can be *officially* expected of church members as they mature and grow.

Thus, the questions we ministers and elders need to ask ourselves are: What vision do we wish to give our people, from the most recent convert to the long-established church member? Do we want them to think that a six- or ten-point doctrinal statement is all that the mature Christian needs to believe and understand? Or do we want to set before them a more ambitious aspiration, something which comes closer to articulating the whole counsel of God? In this context, a good confession becomes not a stick with which to beat people—the popular image that often grips the mind of many believers—but an exciting map of the territory of biblical truth and something to which to aspire.

This should also lead us to be wary of the role parachurch organizations play in the Christian life. They are to serve the church, not vice versa. Most, if not all, parachurch organizations have relatively minimal doctrinal statements, at least compared to the great confessions of the Reformation era, and most sideline issues such as sacraments and even sometimes key soteriological doctrines such as election in order to provide a basis for transdenominational cobelligerence. There is much to be commended about many of these organizations, but the danger is one of perception: if they become the thing of primary importance, rather than the church, then the great confessional distinctives of the church are functionally relativized as things of no real consequence. This has the same practical impact upon church pedagogical expectations as churches themselves having minimal doctrinal statements. It is thus crucial that parachurch involvement is kept in perspective by church leaders and by elders: it can be a helpful and encouraging activity but it should not supplant the absolute priority of the local church and of the denomination, for only in these contexts do we find New Testament governance and appropriate elaboration of the whole counsel of God. The old saying, "What you save them with is what you save them to" may well be an overstatement, but it contains enough truth for us to take it seriously and to reflect upon the role that doctrinal minimalism (at least by confessional standards) can come to play within established churches.

Creeds and Confessions Relativize the Present

We noted above that creeds and confessions can help focus the mind of the church on matters of perennial interest because if something has proved significant over the centuries, one can have a reasonable degree of confidence that it is of importance to more than just this day and generation. This, of course, is another way of saying that creeds and confessions relativize the present. This notion is commendable for at least two reasons.

First, as noted, creeds and confessions that have proved useful over the centuries are clearly immune to the passing fads and tastes of the present. They speak to issues that the church has found important for generations. Thus, while one might point out the obvious, that, say, the Decrees and Canons of the Council of Trent teach a different understanding of justification from that found in the Lutheran Book of Concord, one would have to agree that both documents witness to the fact that justification is an important biblical doctrine and that all churches need to have some position on the matter.

One frequent objection to historic confessions is, of course, that this actually prevents them from being relevant and from speaking to the current age. Such objections are usually rooted in the belief that our knowledge of what the Bible teaches has developed to the point where specific doctrines in the confessional documents are no longer biblically credible. This is a serious matter. Central to the notion of confessionalism is that the confessional documents are themselves a normed norm and always subject to correction by the norming norm, a role reserved for Scripture alone. Given this, confessional revision must always be a possibility; this will be discussed in the appendix.

The second aspect of this advantage of creeds and confessions is that it is profoundly countercultural in a biblical way. What confessionalism does is signal to the church and to the world that the past is in many ways as important, if not more so, than the present. By reciting a creed in the worship service or adhering to a historic confession as part of a congregation's identity, the church makes a powerful statement of her relationship to the contemporary culture. Yes, the present is where we all live and breathe, eat and drink; but the creeds and confessions of the church connect us to the past and indicate that our identity is rooted in that past. This is in line with the thrust of biblical teaching. We noted earlier that Exodus 12 roots the identity of Israel in the present in the recollection of God's mighty acts of salvation in the past. And we also saw that Paul's charge to Timothy was not that he should innovate or take his primary cue from the surrounding culture; rather it was that he should hold fast to the form of sound words that he had been taught by the apostle. Thus, when I took my vows as a minister in the

Orthodox Presbyterian Church and agreed to uphold the teaching of the Westminster Standards, I was effectively saying that the church is bigger than my day and generation; its foundations lie in the past; and I am charged with stewarding that truth in the current context, but that truth neither begins nor ends with me.

Such counterculturalism is important. Theologically, it is vital because salvation is something that was wrought in the past, even as it is applied in the present and will not be fully consummated until some time in the future. Yet there is more to this than straightforward theological significance: it is also important that the church itself cultivate a countercultural culture on this issue; and the liturgical action of using a creed in the worship service and of adhering to a confession as that which defines the church locally and denominationally helps to inculcate precisely such a culture. If the people are saying the Apostles' Creed or the Nicene Creed on a Sunday, if Sunday school classes use the historic confessions as pedagogical guides, and if preachers refer on regular occasion to statements within these documents, then the people will become used to the idea that the church's past is of perennial, vital relevance. The Christian mind is not only doctrinal; it is also marked by a certain attitude to the past. And church practice, as well as church teaching, plays an important role in the cultivation of this.

Creeds and Confessions Help to Define One Church in Relation to Another

Another advantage to holding to a specific confession is that it allows for the clear, public identification of one church in relation to another. As was argued earlier, all churches and all Christians have a functional confession, the difference being whether one writes it down and makes it public or not. Given this, the public nature of confessions can only be a good thing, as it serves the interests of transparency and ecumenism.

It serves transparency because it allows those outside to see what a particular church represents. If someone is on vacation in a town with which they are not familiar, or if someone moves to a new area, it is of immense help to be able to identify clearly where the various churches in the locale stand in relation to various issues. To be told "our church just holds to the Bible" might appear to be rooted in a high view of Scripture but in fact tells the outsider little about the church beyond its generic commitment to some form of biblical authority. It could be a thoroughly orthodox church or it could be an off-the-wall, snake-handling group to whom all notions of God as Trinity might be utterly alien. Unless one attends the church over a period of time, its cherished doctrinal commitments and distinctives will probably not be immediately apparent (snake handling being, I assume, an obvious exception).

Further, such transparency does not only serve the visitor or potential new member; it also serves the local church. When someone visits the congregation, it is useful for congregants to be able to point them to a succinct summary of the church's position on key doctrinal topics. A historic confession would seem to be the most obvious candidate for such a role. It is convenient, honest, and transparent. It leaves nobody in any doubt about what the church is and what she teaches.

Creeds and Confessions Are Necessary for Maintaining Corporate Unity

As noted in chapter 1, we live in an age that fears exclusion, and with good reason. The twentieth century in Europe was one marked from beginning to end by the terrifying results of exclusion. From the Armenian genocide of 1915 through the Holocaust to the ethnic cleansing of the Balkan states in the 1990s, the impact of excluding people, of deciding that this or that group did not belong, was bloody, violent, and undeniable. In the latter part of that century, this no doubt played a part in the rise of philosophies devoted to unmasking how such thinking operated at various levels in society. We also entered a period of Western history where the very idea that one group did not belong, or was somehow inferior to another group, became a profoundly distasteful and disturbing notion.

The impact of this attitude on the church is significant. After all, only a fool would deny that churches have themselves a poor record on exclusion, with many playing collaborative roles in the various persecutions and massacres of history. From the Inquisition to apartheid, churches have often been part of the problem, not the solution. We noted earlier that this has led to a reaction against any kind of exclusionary aspect of church and, inevitably, to a downplaying of doctrinal distinctiveness. The phrases "love unites, doctrine divides," and its close relative, "belonging before believing," are both symptomatic of this yearning for inclusiveness.

There is a tragic irony in this contemporary desire to set belonging and believing somewhat in opposition, with priority being given decisively to the former as a precondition of the latter. First, Paul's theology contains no sense of the two being separable in such a way that allows this kind of opposition to exist. Belonging and believing would seem in Paul's world to be two sides of the same coin. Thus, as we noted in chapter 2, Paul himself characterizes deviation from true doctrine as divisive. We might therefore say that to cease to believe is one and the same with ceasing to belong. That has a distasteful ring to modern ears, for all of the reasons noted above; but it is unavoidable as a conclusion if we take Paul seriously. And given that we are routinely familiar with other institutions where exclusion is part and parcel of good institutional health—from professional societies to political parties—we should not allow religion's past to blunt our understanding and application of Paul's teaching.

Second, while Christianity cannot be reduced to doctrine, to mere teaching, it cannot be meaningfully separated from it either. Even the most basic claims, such as "Jesus is Lord," carry clear doctrinal content that needs to be explicated in a world where, as we have noted before, every heretic has his text and not all who cry "Lord! Lord!" actually have any real saving knowledge of God. That this will inevitably involve exclusion is indisputable. That is another reason why setting the bar low for membership is important, on the grounds that membership is made as inclusive as the Bible allows. But it is also important that membership is as exclusive as the Bible demands, and that means that some will not belong because they do not believe.

The use of confessions as standards of what the church believes and of creeds as corporate expressions of belief in worship services is thus important for underscoring what the church is. If you want to use a contemporary idiom, you could say that they tell the story of who the church is and thus ground its identity in a theological narrative. If, like me, you are comfortable with more traditional terminology, you might say they define who the church is doctrinally. Either way, creeds and confessions establish boundaries of belonging and, by implication, of exclusion. Both are necessary if the church is to have a meaningful corporate identity and unity. Sometimes this will sadly manifest itself in the expulsion of somebody who says he belongs but by his words and actions indicates that such is not the case. That is unfortunate but on occasion necessary. More often, however, the unity will manifest itself in a positive way: the congregation reciting (and rejoicing in) the words of the Apostles' Creed on a Sunday morning; new Christians affirming their belief before the congregation by taking the same vows as the other members have done before them; and worship services marked by a common vocabulary on the lips of all members as they praise their common Lord.

Conclusion

At the end of this chapter, I have little more to add to what I have already said. Each of the above points is grounded in the apostle Paul's concern for the health of the church through her careful steward-ship of God's truth, the handing of that down from generation to generation, and the constant rejoicing in the same, which is meant to characterize the Christian life both at a corporate level and for the individual. Perhaps creeds and confessions are not the only way to do this, but they have certainly been the means of choice for so doing for the majority of Christians since the close of the apostolic era, from the Rule of Faith to the present day. If the churches whose cry is "No creed but the Bible!" are capable of doing the same, history provides little evidence of this, and, for me, the old adage about why one would wish to reinvent the wheel comes into play at this point. There may be ways of doing the above better; but I am unaware of them. And, indeed, the church throughout history has been unaware of them too.

Conclusion

I started this book by highlighting the instance of a pastor who stood up in his pulpit, held the Scriptures aloft, and declared that the Bible and the Bible alone was his creed. As I pointed out then, and have demonstrated in subsequent chapters, that claim was both naive and incorrect. All Christians have a creed or a confession; all Christians think the Bible means something and that its teaching can be summarized in a different form to that in which it was originally given. The only difference is whether one writes the confession down, so that others may scrutinize it and judge whether its teaching is consistent with Scripture, or whether one refuses to do so, in which case one's beliefs are essentially identified with the teaching of Scripture and placed above such scrutiny. Ironically, such a move makes one's tradition unassailable even as one accuses those who hold to creeds and confessions of doing the same.

Thus, the claim to have no creed but the Bible is first and foremost specious; but secondly, it is arguably a contradiction in terms. The Bible itself seems to demand the production of something like a creed or confession. The Pauline imperatives of holding fast to a form of sound words and of guarding the apostolic teaching both push the church toward creedal or confessional formulations and documents. We see hints of these in the New Testament and their rapid emergence in the early postapostolic centuries. The challenge to someone who takes the Bible seriously and yet repudiates the notion of creeds and confessions is: how does one fulfill these Pauline mandates with any degree of confidence? It seems to me that, in the absence of any credible alternative, creeds and confessions are imperatives for the church that takes the Bible seriously, not optional extras and certainly not something that can be decried as sinful, wrong, or unbiblical.

A further point that emerges from the history of creeds and confessions, particularly in relation to the Trinitarian and christological debates of the early centuries, is that Christian theology can only exist in a stable form with a certain ineradicable degree of complexity. The claim that "Jesus is Lord!" is a simple enough linguistic construct; but as the church explored that claim, it became clear that a wealth of sophisticated and intricate theology was implied by, and supported and defined, the statement. Creeds and confessions are complex and precise not because their authors were obsessed with details and distinctions but because they were convinced that the claims made by God and for God were such that careful distinctions and precise statement were necessary if orthodoxy was to be articulated and transmitted from place to place and generation to generation.

In light of the above, and of the many other points made in this book (such as the importance of creeds to worship), creeds and confessions remain of paramount importance to those churches which seek to take the Bible and, more importantly, the God of the Bible seriously. We live in strange times, when the most vibrant strands of conservative, orthodox Protestantism are yet moving away from classic churchly confessionalism even while adopting the name of "confession" for the cause.

There are two dangers here: that a new form of mere Christianity gains a foothold in the camp of the orthodox even while presenting itself as something different, and that there will be a divorce of theology from the life of the organized, particular church under the oversight of office-bearers. Both of these stand at odds with Paul's vision for a sophisticated theology expressed by the church in a form of sound words propagated, protected, and passed on by qualified and duly appointed office-bearers. This move must be resisted by the reassertion of the primacy of the church and by the importance of confessions. Only then can the Pauline vision for the Christian life be truly realized.

This all sounds rather negative, I realize. I trust it is not really so. Creeds and confessions at their best present the church with beautiful summaries of biblical teaching, which are designed not simply to preserve the faith but also to be part of the very life of the worshiping community. As we saw above, there is a doxological element in creeds and confessions, an element which is even on occasion directly related to the polemics they contain. To say that God became man is to deny that Christ is a mere man, a point of polemic; but it is also to assert the reality and truth of the most amazing and wonderful act of God's grace in human history. We should remember that as we reflect upon which confessions our churches should use. An impoverished theological confession can ultimately lead only to an impoverished Christian life.

The last few decades have seen some high profile conversions from evangelical churches to Roman Catholicism. It is difficult to generalize, but a couple of themes seem to have emerged as factors in many of these: evangelicalism lacks historical rootedness, and evangelicalism lacks serious doctrinal weight and long-term stability, with its preference for experience, activism, and mere Christianity (whether at the liberal or the conservative end of the evangelical spectrum). I believe there is an alternative to Rome: it is confessional Protestantism. By that, I do not mean the confessional Protestantism that cherry-picks which bits of various Protestant confessions it likes, assembling an eclectic and minimal conservative Protestant consensus. I mean true confessionalism, one that adheres to a particular confession and connects this to a particular church order and polity. That is confessional Protestantism as the Reformers and their successors would have understood it. It is also Christianity as Paul would have understood it: the church, and only the church, is the divine institution, existing by the command and will of God, for the preservation and proclamation of the faith. It also meets both of those perceived lacunae in evangelicalism: it provides historical roots and serious theology.

I hope this book goes some way to persuading those who earnestly wish to follow Paul and to be faithful, biblical Christians, that such is best done in the context of confessional churches. To take the Bible seriously means that creeds and confessions, far from being intrusions into the Christian life, are actually imperatives for the church.

APPENDIX

On Revising and Supplementing Confessions

Given that the Protestant confessions of the sixteenth and seventeenth centuries place themselves under the supreme authority of Scripture, it is obviously a confessional position to hold to the idea that creeds and confessions can be corrected or supplemented. If they are found to be wrong at some point or to fail to articulate the whole counsel of God as needed by the church, they need to be corrected or supplemented with further confessional statements.

Given this rather obvious point, however, the next question is, how should one go about revising or supplementing a church's confessions? Clearly, it is not something that just any individual church member can do: the burden of this book has been that creeds and confessions are churchly documents, the property of the corporate church not the isolated believer.

To take the notion of revision first, we need to bear a number of things in mind when approaching the topic. First, we must remember that creeds and confessions are ecclesiastical documents. They are adopted by churches as their standards of belief and thus take on corporate significance not possessed by other writings. Calvin's *Institutes* are very precious to me and to many in my denomination, but they have no formal status because nobody is required to take vows to uphold their teaching. Debates over how to translate passages in Calvin, or about whether he is right or wrong on a certain point might well be interesting, but they have little or no ecclesiastical significance. Confessions, though, are different: they are corporate documents to which the church is bound by procedural canons, ordination vows, etc. This difference is important when it comes to confessional revision. Any revision must be done by the church, specifically by those in the church charged with ensuring the soundness of her teaching, that is, the elders.

Second, we need to understand that subscribing to a creed or confession does not mean that we believe every phrase in the document was as well expressed as it could have been or that if we wrote it today we would use exactly the same vocabulary and phrasing. As I read through the Westminster Standards once again in preparation for my ordination vows, there were a number of things that I felt could have been expressed more felicitously. Sometimes there were even things that I would regard as significant omissions. For example, Shorter Catechism 4 reads as follows:

What is God?
God is a Spirit, infinite, eternal, and unchangeable, in his being,
    wisdom, power, holiness, justice, goodness, and truth.

Were I to answer that question today, I would certainly include love as part of God's basic identity. Thus, the response as it stands is arguably deficient; yet, when set within the context of the Catechism as a whole, it is clear that the Westminster divines had a solid understanding of God's love and how it drove the economy of salvation. The lack in the answer to question 4 is odd when taken by itself but is compensated for by the whole.

Thus, as I read the Standards in preparation for ordination, I did not make the mistake of confusing the awkwardness or deficiencies of some of the phrasing with fundamental deviations from biblical teaching. Ultimately, I was not subscribing to the idea that the Westminster divines were the greatest theological prose writers. I was subscribing to the fact that they accurately summarized the Bible's teaching on those matters on which they chose to opine in the Standards. Thus, confessional revision is not justified simply on grounds of verbal clumsiness; it is the concepts the words express which is important. We should not propose confessional revision unless we believe the confession is actually wrong in some point.

Third, many creeds and confessions have retained their basic form and matter and yet transcended their original contexts to become the beloved standards of churches all over the world. Thus, any revision to such by one denomination inevitably sets that denomination apart to some extent from others that subscribe to the same standards in their unrevised form. In this way, revision can actually make the documents less ecumenical. The most famous example of this is the addition of the so-called *filioque* clause to the Nicene Creed at the Third Council of Toledo in 589. This was a Western council whose authority to tinker with the text of the Nicene Creed was denied by the churches in the East. The result was a creed that ultimately provided part of the reason for the Western and Eastern churches to split from each other in the so-called Great Schism of 1054.

This was of course the greatest division of its kind in the history of the church. Yet even revisions to less universally accepted creeds and confessions can bring with them ecumenical consequences. American Presbyterianism eschews the right of the civil magistrate to call a church council and denies the Establishment Principle, whereby the magistrate is required to maintain the Christian (Presbyterian) religion; both principles are taught in the original Westminster Standards and are dear to the heart of many a Scottish Presbyterian. The American revision is in line with American constitutional law and philosophy, but it means that American and Scottish Presbyterians are not entirely united in their confessional commitments. If ever there were to be a move toward church union between such, this would no doubt prove something of a stumbling block. That is not to say that the revisions are not legitimate or important, but it is to say that they always come with a practical, ecumenical cost, and so should not be undertaken lightly or without reference to the wider church world.

Finally, we must always remember that our own perspective is limited. We live in an age where we want things quickly, if not instantly, and where we often have a tendency to see the latest thing as the most significant and earth-shattering phenomenon. Very rarely does this prove to be the case. Often time is the only means by which to judge which discoveries or developments are truly significant and which ones are dead ends, overstated, or simply wrong. The Nicene Creed is still doing sterling work after over 1,600 years; that fact should make us very cautious about deciding to abandon it just because the latest trendy evangelical guru or the cutting-edge professor at the local university decides that it is outmoded and needs to be replaced. To be frank, they would need to come up with something that looks as if it will do the same job just as well and just as universally for the next 1,600 years before I would want to consider throwing out that which has served so many so well for so long.

Thus, any process of confessional revision must take account of the following: as confessions are ecclesiastical documents, they can only be revised by the church. In Presbyterian circles, this means by the presbytery and the assembly of the whole church. Second, it must be undertaken in a solemn and serious manner, with significant prayer, careful investigation into the issues, and extended periods of reflection in order to make sure that any change has been very carefully thought through and is indeed necessary, not a mere stylistic modification.

One final point is that the history of confessional revision is not a particularly happy one. By and large, churches that have engaged in extensive revision of their confessional standards have generally revised them in a direction that has proved in the long term to be inimical to orthodoxy and the health of the church. This was certainly the case with the PCUSA, whose 1967 Confession has at best proved useless in the maintenance of Christianity of even the vaguest kind at the denominational level; at worst it embodied anti-orthodox elements which served to accelerate the process of theological decline.[1]

---

[1] This is not to deny that there are congregations and ministers within the PCUSA who have remained orthodox; it is merely to assert that orthodoxy can no longer be guaranteed at a denominational level because of the confessional criteria now in use.

As a result of this, most orthodox churches have generally resisted the temptation of extensive revision of confessional documents and, when revision has been undertaken, it has been done through established church processes. Some have removed relatively peripheral matters, such as the original Westminster Standards' ruling that a man may not marry his dead wife's sister or the identification of the pope as the Antichrist. Others, rather than removing such have passed church law indicating that the church will not enforce such specific clauses in her courts.

When such a change is made by the church, those who are individual officers have, to paraphrase Presbyterian theologian Charles Hodge, three options: they can actively concur with the change; they can passively submit to the change; or they can peaceably withdraw in light of the change. It is, after all, true that confessional churches have not been immune to doctrinal decline or even outright apostasy. That is not the fault of them being confessional, since the same things can be said of nonconfessional churches as well. It is rather a function of the fact that, like all churches, they are staffed and supervised by fallen human beings. Thus, all officers have the right not to have their consciences bound by changes imposed on them by the church relative to the form or content of subscription. What they do not have, however, is the right of permanent protest within the church. Thus, when a change is made, one must support it, submit to it, or withdraw from the particular church or denomination which one considers to have bound one's conscience in a manner one considers illegitimate.

The second issue is that of supplementing confessional material. Should the church be in the business of adding new documents to which her officers must subscribe? Of course, the history of creeds and confessions is in large part the history of precisely such supplementation: Chalcedon supplements Constantinople; the Westminster Confession supersedes the Thirty-Nine Articles. This is thus a tricky matter to which there is no simple right or wrong answer.

My own approach to this is one of extreme caution. Much of the pressure for confessional supplementation over the last few decades has been connected to wider political and social issues. Thus, one hears calls for the church to make statements on racism or apartheid or the environment or poverty. One of the most famous church confessions of the twentieth century, the Barmen Declaration, was produced by the anti-Nazi German Confessing Church in order to oppose the nationalism and anti-Semitism that had infected the so-called German Christians. Barmen is thus the classic example of a document designed to speak prophetically to the church at a key moment in time.

Two things are worth bearing in mind here. First, there is always a place in church life for occasional documents, reports, or statements which make the church's view on a particular topic clear. Opinions may vary as to whether the church should speak directly to political issues, but even churches with a very precise understanding of the church as a spiritual entity will on occasion produce reports on hot theological topics or points where the church is considered to be under most pressure at that moment in time.

Second, there is—or there should be—a difference between occasional statements and confessionally binding documents. For example, the idea of humanity as made in the image of God, as fallen, as redeemed in Christ, and as looking forward to the general resurrection, is a perennial of the church's teaching. These things apply to all people in all times and all places. Statements on racism, the environment, or apartheid are all much more context specific. They lack ecumenical significance in the broadest sense of the word; and if something lacks ecumenical significance, there is arguably no point in making them part of the church's confessional material, however useful they may be as occasional statements.

In addition, supplementation is often the lazy option. For example, I would argue that the Bible's teaching on the nature of humanity, as summarized in the Westminster Standards, is actually quite sufficient for making the point that racism is sinful and wrong. The same is true for one of today's hot button theological topics: the New Perspective on Paul (NPP). Does the church need to supplement confessional statements on justification in order to combat the revised understanding of salvation being proposed by NPP advocates? I would argue no. There may be a need for a church report on the matter, showing how the NPP is out of accord with the church's confessional position, but the statements on justification in the Westminster Standards seem to me to be robust and thorough enough to be applicable in a helpful manner to the question. In other words, just because something is not dealt with explicitly in the Standards does not mean that those same Standards are not an adequate confessional basis for the church to address whatever the matter may be.

Finally, of course, the liberty and ecumenicity argument also applies here: the more documents a church requires one to uphold, the more one finds that it is binding and micromanaging the consciences of officers and, indeed, the more barriers it is erecting between one's own communion and those of other people. It may be that one concludes that both are necessary; but one should only do that after long and very careful thought about not only the theological content but also the ecclesiastical consequences.

For Further Reading

This book has barely scratched the surface of confessions and confessionalism. For those who want to explore the various issues further, there are a number of good books I recommend.

Collections of Confessions

Many creeds and confessions are readily available on the Internet. In book form, the most easily available collection of creeds and confessions, from the ancient church to the nineteenth century, is Philip Schaff, *The Creeds of Christendom I* (Baker, 1966). A more thorough collection of specifically Reformed confessional documents is the projected three-volume set, edited by James T. Dennison Jr., *Reformed Confessions of the 16th and 17th Centuries in English Translation* (Reformation Heritage, 2008–). A good collection of Baptist documents is William L. Lumpkin and Bill J. Leonard, *Baptist Confessions of Faith* (Judson Press, 2011).

The Use of Confessions

The classic work is the nineteenth-century essay by Samuel Miller, *The Utility and Importance of Creeds and Confessions*. A superb collection of essays on the matter of subscription in Presbyterian and Reformed churches is David W. Hall (ed.), *The Practice of Confessional Subscription* (Covenant Foundation, 2001).

Polity

This book has argued for the importance of church polity to the practice of confessionalism. The gold standard on Presbyterian church polity remains that of the Victorian churchman, James Bannerman, *The Church of Christ* (Solid Ground Christian Books, 2009). Other works worth consulting include David W. Hall and Joseph H. Hall, *Paradigms in Polity: Classic Readings in Reformed and Presbyterian Church Government* (Covenant Foundation, 1994); Edmund P. Clowney, *The Church* (IVP Academic, 1995); and Guy Prentiss Waters, *How Jesus Runs the Church* (P&R, 2011). Mark Dever (ed.), *Polity: Biblical Arguments on How to Conduct Church Life* (Center for Church Reform, 2001) is a good collection of historic essays on the church from a Baptist perspective.

Commentaries on Confessional Standards
Most creeds and confessions are the subject of a significant volume of commentary. I list here my favorite entry-level books on key confessions:

Apostles' Creed: J. I. Packer, *Affirming the Apostles' Creed* (Crossway, 2008)

Westminster Confession: Rowland S. Ward, *The Westminster Confession of Faith: A Study Guide* (New Melbourne Press, 1996)

Westminster Shorter Catechism: G. I. Williamson, *The Westminster Shorter Catechism: For Study Classes* (P&R, 2003)

Westminster Larger Catechism: J. G. Vos, *The Westminster Larger Catechism: A Commentary* (P&R, 2002)

The Belgic Confession: Daniel R. Hyde, *With Heart and Mouth: An Exposition of the Belgic Confession* (Reformed Fellowship, 2008)

The Heidelberg Catechism: Kevin DeYoung, *The Good News We Almost Forgot: Rediscovering the Gospel in a 16th Century Catechism* (Moody, 2010)

The Canons of Dordt: Cornelis P. Venema, *But for the Grace of God: An Exposition of the Canons of Dordt* (Reformed Fellowship, 2011)

Thirty-Nine Articles: Gerald Bray, *The Faith We Confess: An Exposition of the Thirty-Nine Articles* (Latimer Trust, 2009)

Baptist 1689: Samuel E. Waldron, *1689 Baptist Confession of Faith: A Modern Exposition* (Evangelical Press, 1989)

Lutheran: Charles P. Arand, *That I May Be His Own: An Overview of Luther's Catechisms* (Concordia, 2000)

Index